Price Elizabeth, Edward Hailstone

The new book of cookery or every woman a perfect cook

containing the greatest variety of approved receiptsz. in all the branches of cookery and confectionary: boiling, roasting, broiling, frying, stewing, hashing, baking, fricassees, ragouts

Price Elizabeth, Edward Hailstone

The new book of cookery or every woman a perfect cook
containing the greatest variety of approved receiptsz. in all the branches of cookery and confectionary: boiling, roasting, broiling, frying, stewing, hashing, baking, fricassees, ragouts

ISBN/EAN: 9783741183508

Manufactured in Europe, USA, Canada, Australia, Japa

Cover: Foto ©Gila Hanssen / pixelio.de

Manufactured and distributed by brebook publishing software (www.brebook.com)

Price Elizabeth, Edward Hailstone

The new book of cookery or every woman a perfect cook

THE NEW BOOK of COOKERY;
OR,
Every Woman a perfect Cook:

CONTAINING THE
GREATEST VARIETY OF APPROVED RECEIPTS
IN ALL THE BRANCHES OF
COOKERY AND CONFECTIONARY,
VIZ.

BOILING,	RAGOUTS,	CUSTARDS,	PRESERVING,
ROASTING,	MADE-DISHES,	CHEESE-	CANDYING,
BROILING,	SOUPS,	CAKES,	DRYING,
FRYING,	SAUCES,	CREAMS,	POTTING,
STEWING,	PUDDINGS,	SYLLABUBS,	COLLARING,
HASHING,	PIES,	JELLIES,	ENGLISH-
BAKING,	TARTS,	JAMS,	WINES, &c.
FRICASSEES,	CAKES,	PICKLING,	&c. &c. &c. &c.

TO WHICH ARE ADDED,
The best Instructions for Marketing, and Sundry
MODERN BILLS OF FARE;
Also Directions for Clear Starching, and the Ladies Toilet, or
ART OF PRESERVING AND IMPROVING BEAUTY:
Likewise a Collection of PHISICAL RECEIPTS for Families, &c.

The Whole calculated to assist the PRUDENT HOUSEWIFE and her Servants, in furnishing the CHEAPEST and MOST ELEGANT Set of Dishes in the various Departments of COOKERY, and to instruct Ladies in many other Particulars of great Importance too numerous to mention in this Title Page.

By Mrs. ELIZ. PRICE, of BERKELEY-SQUARE,
Assisted by others who have made the Art of Cookery their constant Study.

A NEW EDITION FOR THE PRESENT YEAR,
WITH GREAT ADDITIONS.

Here you may quickly learn with Care
To act the Housewife's Part,
And dress a Modern Bill of Fare
With Elegance and Art.

LONDON:
PRINTED FOR THE AUTHORESS,
And Sold by ALEX. HOGG, No. 16, PATERNOSTER ROW;
and may be had of all other Booksellers.
[*Price only One Shilling.*]

N. B. Mrs: PRICE *respectfully informs the Ladies, and the Public in general, that all similar Publications offered under the Title of her* NEW BOOK OF COOKERY *are spurious, unless bearing her Signature and that of the Publisher, whom she has appointed the only Wholesale Vender of her* NEW BOOK OF COOKERY, *or* Every Woman a perfect Cook.

Eliz: Price

Alexr. Hogg

TO THE PUBLIC.

Having, by a long courſe of practice, acquired, as I flatter myſelf, a conſiderable knowledge in the whole Art of Cookery, I at length determined to commit my obſervations to writing, and publiſh them to the world. I was confirmed in this reſolution by the repeated ſolicitations of many of my friends, who having peruſed the following receipts while they were yet in manuſcript, were pleaſed to expreſs their approbation of them in the higheſt terms of applauſe. I likewiſe ſubmitted this performance to the inſpection of ſeveral eminent men and women cooks, who unanimouſly agreed in recommending it as one of the *moſt uſeful Compendiums of the Art of Cookery* that have appeared in this kingdom; and declared that all the receipts were formed on ſuch a plan, as to unite *œconomy* with *elegance*. Induced by theſe flattering recommendations, and convinced of the utility of an *improved* work of this kind, I have ventured to ſubmit my performance, with all due deference and reſpect, to the judgment of the Public, but particularly to the Ladies, at whoſe hands I reſt in full hopes of candid treatment.

TO THE PUBLIC.

To render this Book the more *extensively useful*, I have added a small collection of the most approved physical receipts, which, upon repeated trials, have been found peculiarly efficacious in the respective disorders to which they have been applied. The Reader will likewise find (besides a variety of receipts in every branch of Cookery) complete instructions for Marketing, several modern Bills of Fare, the Art of Clear-Starching, various Receipts in Confectionary, some choice and valuable Directions for preserving and improving Beauty, &c. &c. In short, I have exerted my utmost endeavours to render this performance as complete as possible, and humbly hope that it will meet with a favourable reception, as it treats of an art which deservedly claims the attention of the Ladies in general, and of Maid-Servants in particular, who, by a careful perusal of the following sheets, will soon become perfectly accomplished in the whole Art of Cookery.

ELIZ. PRICE.

Berkley-Square.

THE

THE
New Book of Cookery,
FOR THE PRESENT YEAR.
INCLUDING
The Newest Improvements on the Subject.

CHAP. I.
OF BOILING.

Rules and Directions necessary to be previously observed in Boiling.

WITH regard to the time sufficient for boiling any kind of meat, it is generally best to allow a quarter of an hour for every pound, when the joint is put into boiling water. Take particular care that your pot be very clean, and skim it well; for otherwise the scum will stick to your meat and make it look black. All sorts of fresh meat you must put in when the water boils; but salt meat when it is cold.

To boil Veal.

Let there be a good fire when the meat is put in, and as soon as the scum begins to rise, take it clear off. A knuckle of veal takes more boiling than any other joint in proportion to its weight: for this obvious reason, because all the gristles ought to be boiled soft and tender. Some cooks put a little milk in the pot with veal, to make it white. Boiled veal may either be sent to table with bacon and greens, or with parsley and butter.

To boil Mutton or Beef.

Having put in your meat, be careful to skim it well, for a scum will rise on every thing that is boiled.

A thick

A thick piece of beef, of twelve or thirteen pounds weight, will take about two hours and a half after the pot boils, if it is put in when the water is cold.

When the meat is boiled, you may serve it up with carrots, potatoes, greens, or turnips. A leg or loin of mutton may likewise be accompanied with melted butter and capers.

To boil a Leg of Lamb, with the Loin fried about it.

Boil the leg about an hour, cut the loin into steaks, beat them with a cleaver, fry them nice and brown, and stew them a little in strong gravy; you must then put the leg in the dish, lay the steaks round it, place some stewed spinach and crisp parsley on each steak, pour on the gravy, and serve up the whole with gooseberry sauce.

To boil a Leg of Pork.

After it has lain in salt six or seven days, put it into the pot to boil, and take care that the fire be very good all the while it is dressing; because it ought to be fully boiled, and requires half an hour more boiling than a leg of veal of the same weight. It is generally accompanied with a peas-pudding, mustard, buttered turnips, greens, or carrots.

To boil Pickled Pork.

Having washed the pork, and scraped it clean, put it in when the water is cold, or, as some say, when the water boils: if a piece of a middling size, an hour will boil it; if a very large piece an hour and a half, or two hours. It will turn to a jelly if kept too long it the pot.

To boil a Tongue.

If the tongue be a dry one, steep it in water all night, and then let it boil three hours: if it be just out of pickle, you may soak it three hours in cold water, and after that boil it till it becomes fit to peel.

To boil a Haunch of Venison.

First let the haunch continue in salt for a week, and then boil it with some turnips, young cabbages, a cauliflower,

Of BOILING.

liflower, and beet-roots; and when you have put your venison in the dish, let the vegetables be difpofed in feparate plates round it, and then you may ferve it up at table.

To boil a Ham.

After putting your ham into the copper, let it be about three or four hours before it boils, and keep it well fkimmed all the time: if it is a fmall one, an hour and a half is fufficient to boil it, after the copper has begun to boil; and, if a large one, it will require two hours.— When you have taken it up, ftrip off the fkin, rub the ham all over with the contents of an egg, ftrew crumbs of bread on it, bafte it with butter, and fet it to the fire till it becomes a light brown; then, if it is to be eat hot, you may garnifh the difh with carrots, and fend it up.

To boil a Calf's Head.

Pick the head very clean, and foak it in water fome time before you put it into the pot; the brains muft then be tied up in a rag, and put in at the fame time with the head, together with a piece of bacon.—When it is done enough you may grill it before the fire, and ferve it up with bacon and greens, and with the brains mafhed and beat up with a little butter, vinegar, pepper, and falt, or lemon, parfley, and fage, in a feparate plate, and the tongue flit and laid in the fame plate.

To boil a Turkey.

Firft draw and trufs your turkey, and cut down the breaft-bone with a knife, then few up the fkin again: the breaft may be filled with ftuffing prepared in the following manner: boil a veal fweet-bread, and chop it fine, with fome lemon-peel, part of the liver, a handful of bread-crumbs, a little beef-fuet, and one or two fpoonfuls of cream, with two eggs, nutmeg, falt, and pepper.— Mix all thefe ingredients together, and ftuff the turkey with part of the ftuffing; the reft may be boiled or fried, and laid round it: dredge your turkey with flour, and having tied it up in a cloth, boil it with milk and water. An hour and a quarter will be sufficient for boiling it, provided it be a young one. For sauce, take a little water or mutton gravy, an onion, a piece of lemon-peel, a bit of thyme, a blade of mace, and an anchovy; let all these be boiled together, and strained through a sieve; add to them some melted butter: then lay round the dish a few sausages fried, and garnish with slices of lemon.

N. B. Some make use of oyster sauce with a boiled turkey.

To boil a Goose.

Having seasoned the goose with pepper and salt for five or six days, let it boil about an hour. Serve it up hot with turnips, carrots, cauliflowers, or cabbage. The sauce for a boiled goose may be either onions or cabbage, first boiled, and then stewed in butter a few minutes.

To boil a Duck.

Draw and scald your duck, and having put it in an earthen pot, pour over it a pint of hot milk, in which it may lie two or three hours; after that dredge it well with flour, put it in a copper of cold water, and let it boil slowly for twenty minutes, then take it out and smother it with onion sauce.

To boil Fowls or Chickens.

Put your chickens in scalding water, pluck and draw them, cut off the heads and necks, and take out the breast-bone; then wash, truss, singe, and flour them; tie them in a napkin, and boil them in milk and water, with a little salt, about twenty-five minutes. You may serve them up with parsley and butter, or with oyster sauce, lemon sauce, &c.

To boil Pigeons with Bacon.

Let your pigeons be plucked, drawn and washed very clean, and then boil them in milk and water by themselves about twenty minutes: in the mean time boil a square piece of bacon, lay it in the middle of your dish,

stew

stew some spinach to put round, and lay the pigeons on the spinach; pour melted butter over them, and garnish them with crisp parsley.

To boil Pigeons with Rice.

After having picked and drawn your pigeons, cut off the pinions and turn the legs under the wings, then put thin slices of bacon, and a large beet-leaf over each pigeon, wrap them in separate cloths and boil them: have ready four ounces of rice boiled soft, put the rice into some veal gravy thickened with flour and butter, and boil it a little in that gravy, adding two or three spoonfuls of cream: then take out the pigeons, leaving the bacon and beet-leaves on them, and serve them up with the rice poured over them.

To boil Snipes and Woodcocks.

Take the snipes and gut them clean, and boil them in good strong broth or beef-gravy; let them be covered close and kept boiling, and ten minutes will be sufficient. Meanwhile chop the guts and liver small, take a little of the gravy in which your snipes are boiling, and stew the guts in it with a blade of mace. Take a few crumbs of bread, and have them ready fried crisp in a little fresh butter. When your snipes or woodcocks are done, add to the guts two spoonfuls of red wine and a small piece of butter rolled in flour; set them on the fire in a saucepan, and shake it well, (but do not stir with a spoon) till the butter is melted; then put in the bread-crumbs, give the saucepan a shake, and pour this sauce over the birds. You may garnish your dish with lemon.

To boil Rabbits.

When you have properly trussed your rabbits, boil them about half an hour, then smother them with onion sauce, pull out their jaw bones and stick them in their eyes, put a sprig of myrtle or barberries in their mouths, and serve them up. Garnish with sliced lemon and barberries.

To boil Rabbits with Sausages.

Boil a couple of rabbits, and before they are quite done, you must put in a pound of sausages to boil with them; when they are done enough, dish them up, and place the sausages round the dish, with a few fried slices of bacon: for sauce, put melted butter and mustard beat up together in a cup.

To boil Pheasants or Partridges.

Let them be boiled in a considerable quantity of water. As for partridges, a quarter of an hour is sufficient to boil them. Half an hour will do a small pheasant, and three quarters a large one. The sauce for a boiled pheasant may be stewed celery thickened with cream, a piece of butter rolled in flour, some grated nutmeg, and a spoonful of white wine. For sauce to a partridge, parboil the liver, and scald some parsley; chop these fine, and put them into some melted fresh butter; then squeeze in a little juice of lemon, and having boiled the whole up, pour it over your partridge.

To boil Sturgeon.

Clean your piece of sturgeon well, and boil it in as much liquor as will just cover it, adding to the water a stick of horse-radish, some whole pepper, two or three pieces of lemon-peel, a pint of vinegar, and a little salt. When it is done serve it up with the following sauce; dissolve an anchovy in a pound of melted butter, bruise the body of a crab in the butter, put in a blade or two of mace, a few shrimps or crawfish, a little catchup and lemon juice, and give the whole a boil up. Garnish with fried oysters, scraped horse-radish, and slices of lemon.

To boil a Skate or Thornback.

First let your skate be well cleaned; then cut it in long narrow pieces, and throw it into salt and boiling water; when it has boiled a quarter of an hour, take it out, slip off the skin, then put it again into the saucepan, with a little vinegar, and when it is done enough,

drain

drain it well, and pour over it fhrimp or mufcle fauce. You may garnifh the difh with barberries and horferadifh.

To boil Flounders and all Kinds of Flat Fifh.

You muft cut off the fins, and nick the brown fide under the head; then gut your fifh and boil them in falt and water: make either fhrimp, cockle, anchovy, or mufcle fauce, and garnifh with red cabbage.

To boil a Frefh Cod.

Having well wafhed and gutted your cod, rub the back-bone with a little falt, and boil it gently till it is done enough. You may ferve it up with anchovy, fhrimp, oyfter, or lobfter fauce, and garnifh with flices of lemon, fcraped horfe-radifh, and fmall fried fifh.

To drefs Salt Cod.

Let it be fteeped in water all night, and boiled the next day: when it is enough, pull it in flakes into the difh, pour over it egg fauce, or parfnips boiled and beat fine, with butter and cream, and fend it to table on a water difh.

To boil a Turbot.

Put a handful of falt into the mouth and belly of the turbot, and lay it in falt and water for two hours before it is dreffed. Then fet on your fifh-kettle with water and falt, a little vinegar, a ftick of horfe-radifh, and a bunch of fweet herbs. When the water boils lay your turbot on a fifh plate, put it into the kettle and boil it gently. Serve it up with anchovy or lobfter fauce, and garnifh the difh with crifp parfley and pickles.

N. B. A turbot of a middling fize will take about twenty minutes boiling.

To boil Mackarel.

Soak them a confiderable time in fpring water, then put them into a ftewpan, with as much water as will cover them, and a little falt: let a fmall bunch of fennel be

boiled

boiled along with them; and when you dish them up, garnish with the roes and the fennel shred fine. The sauce generally used with boiled mackarel is parsley and butter.

To boil Salmon.

After having well scraped and cleansed your salmon from scales and blood, let it lie about an hour in spring water and salt; then put it in the fish kettle, with a suitable quantity of salt and horse-radish, and some sweet herbs. If it be a thick piece, it will take h. lf an hour; if small, twenty minutes. Garnish your dish with scraped horse-radish and fennel, or with fried smelts or gudgeons. The sauce may be melted butter, with or without anchovy, and shrimp or lobster sauce.

To boil Eels.

First skin, gut, and wash your eels, then roll them round with the heads innermost, and run a skewer through them. Boil them in salt and water; serve them up with parsley sauce, and garnish with lemon.

To boil Carp or Tench.

Clean your carp or tench very well, and boil them in a stewpan; mix with the water some salt, whole pepper, horse-radish, sweet herbs, and lemon-peel. For sauce take some of the liquor, a pint of shrimps, a glass of white wine, and an anchovy bruised; boil these together in a saucepan with a piece of butter rolled in flour.

To boil a Cauliflower.

Take off all the green part, cut the flower into four quarters, and let it soak an hour in clean water; then put it into boiling milk and water, or (if you have no milk) into water only, and take care to skim the saucepan well. When the stalks are tender, take out the cauliflower, lay it in a cullender to drain, and serve it up with melted butter. This is, among the generality of people, one of the most favourite plants in the whole kitchen garden.

To boil Broccoli.

First strip off all the little branches till you come to the top one; then with a knife peel off the hard outside skin on the stalks, and throw them into a pan of clean water as you do them. Put them in a stewpan of boiling water, with some salt in it, and let them boil till they are tender. Send them to table with butter in a cup. Some people eat broccoli like asparagus, with toast laid in the dish.

To boil Parsnips.

Let your parsnips be well washed, and boiled till they are soft; then take off the skin, beat them in a bowl with a little salt, and add to them a piece of butter and some cream, put them in a tossing pan, and let them boil till they are like a light custard pudding; you may then lay them on a plate and serve them up.

To boil Artichokes.

Pull off the stalks, and wash the artichokes clean; then put them in a saucepan of cold water, but do not cover them. An hour and a quarter will do them after the water boils. When you dish them up, put butter in tea-cups between each artichoke.

To boil Asparagus.

Having scraped your asparagus, soak them in clean water, tie them in little bundles, and boil them in a stewpan of water with salt in it. Before you take them up, toast a round or two of a quartern loaf, which must be dipped in the boiling water and laid in the bottom of your dish: pour a little butter over the toast, and lay your asparagus on it with the white ends outwards. You need not pour butter over the asparagus, but send it up in a sauce-boat.

To boil Spinach.

You must pick and wash your spinach very clean, then put it in a saucepan that will just hold it, scatter a handful of salt over it, and cover the pan close: don't put any
water

water in, but frequently ſhake your ſaucepan. When you find the ſpinach ſhrunk and fallen to the bottom, and that the liquor which comes out of it boils up, it is done: then ſqueeze it between two plates, and ſerve it up with melted butter in a boat.

To boil Green Peas.

Shell your peas, and put them into boiling water, with a few leaves of mint and a little ſalt: as ſoon as they boil, throw in a ſmall piece of butter, and ſtir them about; when they are enough, ſtrain them in a ſieve, and diſh them up with butter in a cup. Lay a piece of bacon over your peas, and garniſh with mint boiled and chopped fine.

To boil Turnips.

Pare them well; and boil them in the pot with either beef, lamb, or mutton: when they are tender take them out, ſqueeze them between two trenchers, put them in a pan, maſh them with butter and a little pepper and ſalt, and ſend them to table. You may likewiſe ſend them up whole, with ſome melted butter in a baſon, that every one may butter and ſeaſon them to his palate.—N. B. Potatoes may be maſhed in the ſame manner as turnips.

To boil French Beans.

Firſt cut off the ends of your beans, then cut them in two, and afterwards acroſs; put them in ſalt and water as you do them, and let them ſtand an hour: boil them in a great deal of water with a handful of ſalt in it, and take care they do not loſe their fine green. Serve them up with melted butter.

To boil Broad Beans, commonly called Windſor Beans.

When your beans are ſhelled, put them in the pot with ſome picked parſley and ſalt: in the mean time boil a piece of bacon by itſelf, and when you have diſhed up the beans, lay the bacon over them, and ſend parſley and butter in a ſauce-boat. Garniſh with boiled parſley.

CHAP.

CHAP. II.

OF ROASTING.

General Directions with Regard to Roasting.

IN the first place, you must regulate your fire according to the piece of meat you are to dress: if it be a small or thin piece, make a pretty little brisk fire; but if it be a large joint, let a very good fire be laid to cake. Take care to keep your fire always clear, and let your spit be very clean. When the steam draws near the fire, it is a sign the meat is done enough; but you will best judge of that from the time it was put down. Observe that in frosty weather all kinds of meat take more time in dressing.

To roast Mutton.

If it be a chine or saddle of mutton, you must raise the skin, and then skewer it on again; for that will prevent its being scorched. Strip off the skin about a quarter of an hour before you take it up; throw some flour on your meat, together with a handful of salt, and baste it with butter. Roast mutton, when served up, may be accompanied with French beans, broccoli, potatoes, cauliflower, horse-radish, or water-cresses.—N. B. Onion sauce is frequently used with a shoulder of mutton, either roasted or boiled.

To roast Mutton so as to make it eat like Venison.

Having procured a fat hind-quarter of mutton, cut the leg in the shape of haunch of venison, lay it in a pan, and pour over it a bottle of red wine, in which it must lie twenty-four hours; then put it on the spit, and baste it with the same liquor and butter all the time it is roasting. If you have a good quick fire, your meat will be done in two hours. You may send it to table with

with some good gravy in one bason, and currant jelly in another.

To roast a Leg of Mutton with Oysters or Cockles.

Take a leg of mutton that has been butchered two or three days before, stuff it all over with oysters or cockles, and roast it. Garnish the dish with horse-radish.

To roast Beef.

Butter a piece of writing-paper, and fasten it with small skewers to the top of your beef; then lay it down to a good fire, throw some salt on it, and baste it well with good dripping. A little while before you take it up, remove the paper, dredge the meat with some flour, and baste it with a piece of butter. Garnish the dish with scraped horse-radish, and send it to table with broccoli, French beans, potatoes, horse-radish, or cauliflower. When you want to keep your meat a few days before you dress it, you must dry it well with a clean cloth, then flour it all over, and hang it up in a place where the air may come to it.

To roast Veal.

In dressing a fillet or loin of veal, paper the udder of the fillet to preserve the fat, and the back of the loin to prevent it from being scorched. Lay your meat at some distance from the fire till it is soaked, and then draw it nearer the fire; baste it well with butter, and dust it with a little flour. The stuffing for a fillet is made thus: take half a pound of suet, about a pound of grated bread, some parsley, thyme, sweet majoram, and savory, a piece of lemon-peel, nutmeg, pepper, and salt, and mix them up together with the yolks and whites of a few eggs.

A breast of veal must be roasted with the caul on, and the sweet-bread skewered on the back-side: when it is almost done, take off the caul, and baste it with butter and a little flour.

To roaſt Lamb.

When you lay it down, baſte it well with freſh butter, and ſcatter on it a very little flour; then baſte it with what drips from it; and juſt before you take it up, ſprinkle on a little ſalt and chopped parſley, and baſte it again with butter. You may ſerve it up with mint ſauce, green peas, a ſallad, cauliflower, or French beans.

To roaſt a Leg of Lamb with Forcemeat.

Take a large leg of lamb, and with a ſharp knife cut off all the meat, leaving the ſkin whole with the fat on it: then chop the meat ſmall with half a pound of beef ſuet, ſome marrow, a few oyſters, an onion, an anchovy, ſome ſweet herbs, lemon-peel, mace, and nutmeg; and having beat all theſe together in a mortar, ſtuff the ſkin with them, ſew it up, rub it with the yolks of eggs, ſpit it, flour it all over, lay it down to the fire, and baſte it well with butter: when done, pour ſome nice gravy into the diſh, and ſend it up.

To roaſt Pork.

In roaſting a loin of pork, you muſt cut the ſkin acroſs in ſmall ſtreaks, and take care that it be jointed before you lay it down; it is ſometimes ſerved up with onions. —A ſparerib ſhould be roaſted before a clear fire, and baſted with a ſmall piece of butter, a little flour, and ſome ſage ſhred fine: ſend it up with apple ſauce. The knuckle of a roaſt leg of pork is frequently ſtuffed with ſage and onion chopped ſmall, with a little pepper and ſalt, and eat with gravy and apple ſauce. But the beſt way of roaſting a leg is as follows: firſt parboil it, then ſkin it and lay it down, and baſte it with butter; take a little ſage ſhred fine, a few crumbs of bread, ſome nutmeg, pepper, and ſalt; mix theſe together, and ſtrew them over your meat while it is roaſting: ſend up ſome gravy in the diſh, and ſerve it up with apple ſauce and potatoes. A griſkin may be dreſſed in the ſame manner.

N. B. Pork muſt be well done, otherwiſe it is apt to ſurfeit.

To roaſt a Tongue.

You muſt parboil it firſt, then roaſt it; baſte it well with butter, ſtick ten or twelve cloves about it, and ſend it to table with ſome gravy and ſweet ſauce.—N. B. An udder, dreſſed the ſame way, is very good eating.

To dreſs a pickled Neat's Tongue.

Having firſt ſoaked it, boil it till the ſkin will peel off, then ſtick it with cloves, put it on the ſpit, wrap a veal caul over it, and roaſt it till it is enough; after which you muſt take off the caul, and ſerve up your tongue with gravy in the diſh, and ſome veniſon ſauce in a boat. Garniſh with raſpings of bread and ſliced lemon.

To roaſt a Pig.

Put into the belly of your pig a few ſage leaves chopped, a piece of butter, a cruſt of bread grated, and ſome pepper and ſalt; ſew it up, ſpit it, and lay it down to a large briſk fire. Flour it all over very thick, and continue to do ſo till the eyes begin to ſtart. As ſoon as you find the ſkin tight and criſp, and that the eyes are dropped, lay two baſons in the dripping-pan, to receive the gravy that comes from it. When the pig is enough, put a lump of butter into a cloth, and rub all over it, till the flour is quite off; then take it up into your diſh, and having cut off the head, cut the pig in two down the back; chop off the ears, and place one upon each ſhoulder; cut the under jaw in two, and lay one on each ſide; melt ſome butter, put it into the gravy that came from your pig, boil it up and put it into the diſh with the brains bruiſed fine, and a little ſhred ſage; then ſend the whole to table, with bread ſauce in a baſon, and garniſh with lemon.

A Pig barbicued.

Take two or three anchovies, a few leaves of ſage, and the liver of the pig; chop them very ſmall, and put them into a marble mortar, with half a pint of red wine, ſome butter, bread-crumbs, and pepper: beat them all together to a paſte, and ſew them up in your pig's belly; then

then lay it down to the fire, singe it well, pour in the dripping-pan two or three bottles of red wine, and baste it with wine all the time it is roasting. When it is almost done, take the sauce out of your dripping-pan, add to it one anchovy, half a lemon, and a bunch of sweet herbs, boil these a few minutes, then take up your pig, put a small lemon or apple in its mouth, strain your sauce, and pour it on boiling hot; lay barberries and sliced lemon round the pig, and serve it up whole.

To roast a Calf's Liver.

Lard it with bacon, fasten it on the spit, and roast it with a gentle fire: send it to table with good veal gravy, or melted butter.

To roast Venison.

Take a haunch of venison, and when you have spitted it, lay over it a large sheet of white paper, then a thin paste with another sheet of paper over it, and tie it well to prevent the paste from falling. About five or six minutes before you take it up, take off the paper and paste, baste it with butter, and dredge it with a little flour: when you dish it up, let it be accompanied with some good gravy in one sauce boat, and sweet sauce in another. If it be a large haunch, it will take three hours roasting. The neck and shoulder may be dressed the same way. The sauce for venison may be either currant jelly warmed, or half a pint of red wine, with a quarter of a pound of sugar, simmered over a clear fire for seven or eight minutes; or about half a pint of vinegar, with a proportionate quantity of sugar, simmered till it becomes of the consistence of a syrup.

To roast Rabbits.

Having trussed your rabbits, put them down to a quick clear fire, dredge them, baste them well with butter, and roast them near three quarters of an hour: boil the livers with a bunch of parsley, and chop them very fine; then melt some good butter, put into it half the liver and parsley, and pour it in the dish; garnish with the other half. The French sauce for rabbits consists of onions minced small, fried and mixed up with pepper and mustard.—Some people put a pudding in a rabbits belly when they roast it.

To roast a Hare.

Stuff your hare with a pudding made thus: take some crumbs of bread, a quarter of a pound of beef-suet minced fine, the hare's liver parboiled and chopped small, some butter, two or three eggs, one anchovy, a little lemon-peel, parsley, thyme, nutmeg, pepper, and salt; mix these several ingredients together, and put them into the belly of your hare, and then roast it. Put about three pints of milk and half a pound of fresh butter in your dripping-pan, which ought to be very clean: baste the hare with this all the while it is roasting; and when it has soaked up all the butter and milk, it will be done enough. Serve it up with melted butter and cream, currant jelly, gravy, or claret sauce.

Another Way of roasting a Hare.

Take a piece of fat bacon, some bread-crumbs, the liver of a hare, an anchovy, a shalot, some nutmeg and winter-savory; chop these fine, beat them up to a paste, and put them into the hare; then lay it down to the fire, baste it with stale beer, put a small piece of bacon in the dripping-pan, and when it is half roasted, baste it with butter: send it to table with melted butter and savory.

To roast a Turkey.

You must take a pound of veal cut small, half a pound of beef-suet chopped, some parsley, thyme, and savory, two cloves, a bit of lemon-peel, half a nutmeg grated, some mace, pepper, and salt, the yolks of two eggs, and a sufficient quantity of grated bread; mix the whole together and stuff the craw of your turkey with it; then paper the breast, and having spitted the turkey, lay it down at a proper distance from the fire, singe it with white paper, dust on some flower and baste it with butter.

butter. When it is enough fend it up with fome good beef gravy in a difh, and either onion, bread, celery, or oyfter fauce in a boat. Garnifh with lemon and pickles.

N. B. A fmall turkey will take three quarters of an hour in roafting; a middling one a full hour; a very large one, an hour and a half. A full grown goofe will take an hour; a large fowl three quarters of an hour; a middle fize fowl half an hour; a fmall chicken twenty minutes; a tame duck of a middling fize takes about half an hour; a wild one, fifteen or twenty minutes: but this depends entirely on the goodnefs or flacknefs of your fire.

To roaft a Goofe or a Duck.

Chop a few fage leaves and one or two onions, mix them with fome butter, pepper, and falt, and put them into the belly of your goofe or duck; then fpit it and lay it down, finge it well, dredge it with flour, and bafte it with frefh butter. When you difh up your goofe, fend gravy in one bafon, and apple-fauce in another. Pour fome gravy in the difh with your duck, and fend up onion fauce in a boat.

The fauce for a roafted green goofe is made thus: take fome melted butter, put into it a fpoonful of the juice of forrel, a little fugar, and a few coddled goofe-berries; then pour it in your fauce-boat, and ferve it up hot.

To roaft Fowls or Chickens.

Having drawn and truffed your fowls, lay them down to a good fire, finge, dredge, and bafte them well with butter: ferve them up with gravy in the difh, and either egg, bread, fhalot, or oyfter fauce in a bafon.

To roaft a Fowl or Turkey with Chefnuts.

Take a quarter of a hundred chefnuts, roaft and peel them; bruife about a dozen of them in a mortar, with the liver of the fowl a quarter of a pound of ham, and fome fweet herbs; mix thefe together with fome mace, pepper, falt, and nutmeg, and having put them into your fowl, fpit and roaft it, and bafte it with butter. For sauce, take the rest of the chesnuts, chop them small, and put them into some strong gravy, with a glass of white wine, and a piece of butter rolled in flour: pour the sauce in the dish, and garnish with water-cresses and sliced orange.

To roast Wild Ducks, Widgeons, or Teal.

If your fire be very good and brisk, a teal, wild duck, or widgeon will be done in a quarter of an hour. The following sauce will suit all kinds of wild fowl: take a sufficient quantity of veal-gravy, season it with pepper and salt, squeeze in a little claret, and the juice of two oranges.

To roast Pheasants or Partridges.

Lay them down at a good distance from the fire, dredge them, and baste them with nice butter, that they may go to table with a fine froth: they will take twenty minutes or half an hour roasting: when you dish them up, let there be some gravy in the dish, and bread or celery sauce in a boat. Garnish with slices of oranges or lemon.

N. B. You may, if you please, lard turkeys, partridges, pheasants, larks, ortolans, &c. when you roast them.

To roast Pigeons.

Stuff them with a piece of butter, some chopped parsley, pepper, and salt; then put them on a small spit, flour them, and baste them with butter: they will be done in fifteen or twenty minutes. Many people roast them by a string fastened to the top of the chimney-piece. When they are enough, lay them in the dish, and put bunches of asparagus round them, with parsley and butter for sauce.

To roast Larks.

Put your larks upon a long skewer, then tie the skewer to a spit, and let them roast ten or twelve minutes at a quick clear fire: baste them with good butter, and
strew

strew over them a few crumbs of bread mixed with flour: then fry some bread-crumbs with a piece of butter, and lay them in the dish round your birds. Send up gravy in a boat, and garnish with sliced orange. Ortolans may be dressed the same way.

To roast Snipes or Woodcocks.

Truss your snipes, and put them on a small bird-spit; dredge them, and baste them well with butter: have ready a slice of bread toasted brown, which must be laid in a dish, and set under the birds while they are roasting. They will take a quarter of an hour or twenty minutes. When they are done, take them up, and lay them on the toast; pour some beef-gravy and melted butter in the dish, and garnish with orange or lemon.

N. B. You need not draw a woodcock or snipe when you roast it.

To roast Quails.

Let them be stuffed with beef-suet and sweet herbs chopped and seasoned with a little spice: spit them, and when they begin to grow warm, baste them with salt and water; then flour them, and baste them with a little butter. Meanwhile dissolve an anchovy in good gravy, with two or three shalots chopped small, and the juice of a Seville orange; dish up your quails in this sauce, and garnish with lemon and fried bread-crumbs.

To roast a large Eel.

Skin your eel, scour it well with salt, gut, wash, and dry it; scotch it on both sides, rub it over with yolks of eggs, and stuff its belly with a forcemeat made of suet, sweet herbs, a shalot, pepper, salt and nutmeg: then draw the skin over it, and fasten it on the spit; baste it with butter, and serve it up with anchovy sauce.

To roast Sturgeon.

Take a piece of fresh sturgeon, let it lie six or eight hours in water and salt: then spit and lay it down, baste it with flour and butter, strew over it some grated nutmeg,

meg, a little beaten mace, pepper, and salt, a few crumbs of bread, and some sweet herbs powdered fine. When your sturgeon is done, dish it up, and garnish with slices of lemon. For sauce, take a pint of water, a bit of lemon peel, an onion, an anchovy, a bunch of sweet herbs, some horse-radish, mace, cloves, and whole pepper; let this mixture boil a quarter of an hour, then strain it, put it again into the saucepan, with a pint of white wine, a few oysters, the inside of a crab or lobster bruised fine, two or three spoonfuls of catchup and walnut pickle, and a lump of butter rolled in flour; boil the whole up together, and pour it over the fish.

To roast a Lobster.

First parboil your lobster, then rub it well with butter, and set it before the fire; baste it all over till the shell looks of a dark brown colour, and serve it up with melted butter in a bason.

To roast a Pike.

Having gutted and cleaned your pike, take a few crumbs of bread, some beef suet, chopped parsley, thyme, savory, mace, nutmeg, salt, and pepper, and mix them up with raw eggs and a piece of butter; make the whole into a long pudding, and put it in the belly of your fish: then put two laths on each side of the pike, and fix it on the spit; and while it is roasting, baste it with anchovies dissolved in butter. Send it to table with anchovy or oyster sauce, and garnish with lemon.

CHAP. III.

OF BROILING, FRYING, STEWING, HASHING, and BAKING.

BROILING.

To broil Steaks.

TAKE care that you have a clear brisk fire when you broil any thing, and that your gridiron be very clean. Lay your steaks on the gridiron, and sprinkle a little pepper and salt over them. If they are beef steaks, you need not turn them till one side is done; but if they are mutton or pork steaks, they must be frequently turned. When they are enough, take them off the gridiron very carefully, that none of the gravy may be lost; lay them in a hot dish, rub them well with butter, and mix with the gravy an onion or shalot chopped as small as possible. The general sauce for steaks is, horse-radish for beef, pickles for mutton, and mustard for pork.

To broil Chickens.

You must slit them down the back, season them with pepper and salt, and lay them on a very clear fire, at a good distance: let the inside lie downwards till it is above half done; then turn them, and be careful that the fleshy side do not burn; scatter over them some fine raspings of bread, and let them be of a fine brown. For sauce send up good gravy with mushrooms, and garnish your dish with lemon, and the livers and gizzards broiled.

To broil the Tongues of Sheep or Hoggs.

Boil the tongues first, then blanch and split them, season them with salt and pepper, dip them in eggs, strew some crumbs of bread on them, broil them till they

they are brown, and fend them to table with a little gravy and butter.

To broil Pigeons.

When you have picked and drawn your pigeons, you muſt ſplit them down the back, and having ſeaſoned them with a little pepper and ſalt, lay them on the gridiron, rub them over with butter, and keep turning them till they are done; then diſh them up, pour over them either gravy or melted butter, and garniſh with criſped parſley.

To broil Eels.

Having ſkinned and cleanſed your eels, rub them with the yolk of an egg, ſtrew over them chopped parſley, ſage, pepper, ſalt, and bread crumbs, lay them on your gridiron, and when they are enough ſerve them up with parſley and butter, or anchovy ſauce.

To ſpitchcock Eels.

Split a large eel down the back, joint the bones, and cut it in two or three pieces; put a little vinegar and ſalt in ſome melted butter, in which your eel muſt lie three or four minutes; then take the pieces up one by one, turn them round on a thin ſkewer, roll them in crumbs of bread, and broil them of a fine brown: lay them on your diſh with plain melted butter, and fried parſley for garniſh.

To broil Salmon, Cod, Whitings, Haddocks, Mackarel, or Weavers.

Have a quick clear fire, and ſet your gridiron high; then flour your fiſh, and broil them of a good brown. For ſauce take ſome melted butter, with the body of a lobſter bruiſed in it, and pour it in your diſh, or into a ſauce boat. Garniſh with ſliced lemon and horſe-radiſh.

N. B. You may, if you like it, ſtuff mackarel when you broil them.

To broil Cod-Sounds.

Let them lie a few minutes in hot water; then rub them

them well with salt, take off the black dirty skin, put them in a saucepan, and let them simmer till they begin to be tender; take them out, sprinkle on them some flour, salt, and pepper, and lay them on the gridiron; serve them up with melted butter and mustard.

To broil Herrings.

Scale, gut, and wash your herrings, cut off their heads, dry them in a cloth, notch them across with a knife, flour and broil them. In the meantime take the heads that you cut off, mash them, and boil them a quarter of an hour in ale or small beer, with an onion or some whole pepper; then strain this mixture and thicken it with butter, mustard, and flour: pour this sauce into a boat, and send it up with the herrings.

FRYING.

To fry Beef Steaks.

Beat your steaks well, and fry them in half a pint of good ale; whilst they are frying, take a large onion cut small, some grated nutmeg, pepper, and salt, and a little parsley and thyme shred fine; roll all together in a piece of butter, and then in a little flour; put this into the frying-pan, and give it a shake. When the sauce is of a proper thickness, and the steaks are tender, you may dish them up and send them to table.

Another Method of frying Beef Steaks.

You must cut the lean by itself, and fry it in as much butter as will just moisten the pan; pour out the gravy as it runs from the meat, and turn your steaks frequently; then fry the fat by itself, and lay it upon the lean steaks: add to the gravy a glass of red wine, half an anchovy, a shalot chopped small, some pepper, salt, and nutmeg; give it a boil up, pour it over the steaks, and serve them up.

To fry Mutton Chops.

First take a few crumbs of bread, a piece of lemon-peel shred fine, a little chopped thyme and parsley, with some nutmeg, pepper and salt; then cut a loin of mutton into steaks, beat them well, and rub them all over with the yolks of two or three eggs. Fry your steaks of a nice brown, and while they are frying, strew on them the bread crumbs, &c. Let your sauce be good gravy, with a small anchovy in it, and two or three spoonfuls of claret.

To fry Veal Cutlets.

Lard them with slips of bacon, wash them over with eggs, and strew on them some grated lemon peel, bread crumbs, sweet herbs, salt, pepper, and nutmeg, and fry them in good butter. When you dish them up, pour some hot gravy over them; and garnish with lemon and pickles.

To fry cold Veal.

Cut your veal into very thin pieces, dip them in the yolk of an egg, and after that in crumbs of bread, with a few sweet herbs and shred lemon peel in it; then grate some nutmeg over them, and fry them in fresh butter. Meanwhile make a little gravy of the bone of the veal; and when your meat is fried, lay it in a dish before the fire; then throw some flour into the pan, stir it round, put in the gravy, squeeze in it a little lemon juice, and pour it over the veal. Garnish with slices of lemon.

To fry Lamb Steaks.

Having cut a loin of lamb into thin steaks, season them with pepper, salt, and nutmeg, and fry them with good butter. When they are enough lay them in a dish before the fire, that they may keep hot; then pour out the butter, scatter a little flour on the bottom of the pan, put in a quarter of a pint of boiling water, and a lump of butter; shake the whole together, boil it up, pour it upon your steaks, and serve them up.

To fry Tripe.

You muſt cut your tripe into pieces of about the length of three inches, dip them in bread crumbs and the yolk of an egg, and fry them of a good brown; then take them out of the frying-pan, and lay them in a diſh to drain: ſend them to table with melted butter and muſtard in a baſon.

To fry Sweetbreads and Kidneys.

When you have ſplit the kidneys, fry them and the ſweetbreads in butter; ſerve them up with muſhroom ſauce, and garniſh your diſh with lemon and fried parſley.

To fry Sauſages.

Cut them in ſingle links, and fry them in good butter; then take a round of a loaf, fry it of a nice brown in the ſame butter, and lay it in the bottom of your diſh; put the ſauſages on the toaſt in four parts, lay poached eggs between them, and diſh them up with melted butter.

To fry Sauſages with Apples.

Take ſix apples, and half a pound of ſauſages; cut four of the apples into thin ſlices, and quarter the other two; then fry them with the ſauſages, and when they are enough, lay the ſauſages in the middle of your diſh, and the ſliced apples round them. Garniſh with the quartered apples.

To make Scotch Collops.

Cut ſome veal in ſmall thin collops, beat them well with a rolling pin, dip them in the yolks of eggs, grate ſome nutmeg over them, and fry them in a little butter till they are of a fine brown; then pour the butter from them, put in the pan half a pint of gravy, a few muſhrooms, a glaſs of white wine, a piece of butter rolled in flour, a little cream, and the yolks of two eggs; and ſtir it all together with your meat. When the collops are done, put them in your diſh, pour the ſauce on them, lay over them ſome forcemeat balls, and little ſlices of bacon, and garniſh with lemon.—N. B. If you would have the collops white, you must neither dip them in eggs, nor fry them brown.

To fry Calf's Liver and Bacon.

Slice the liver, and fry it nice and brown, then fry the bacon; lay the liver in your dish, and the bacon upon it; serve them up with gravy and butter mixed with the juice of an orange or lemon, and garnish the dish with lemon cut in slices.

To fry Flat Fish.

Dry them well in a cloth, flour them, and rub them over with the contents of an egg; fry them either in oil, butter, hog's lard, or dripping, and let them be of a fine light brown. Send them to table with melted butter, or what sauce you please.

To fry Carp or Tench.

First scale, gut, and wash them, then sprinkle them with salt, flour them, and fry them in clarified butter. Serve them up with whatever fish sauce you like, and garnish with lemon, crisp parsley, and fried sippets.— N. B. Tench are sometimes fried with forcemeat.

To fry Herrings.

When you have cleaned your herrings well, dust them with a little flour, and fry them in dripping or butter: send them up with butter and mustard in a bason, or with the same sauce that I have before directed for broiled herrings. Garnish your dish with the roes and onions fried.

To fry Trout.

Having scaled, gutted, washed, and dried your trout, flour them, and fry them of a fine brown, either with butter, dripping, or suet: dish them up with anchovy sauce, or plain melted butter, and garnish with sliced lemon and crisped parsley. You may fry perch, small pikes, gudgeons, roach, smelts, and other small fish in the same manner.

To fry Eels.

Skin and clean your eels, split them and cut them in pieces; let them lie two or three hours in a pickle composed of vinegar, lemon juice, pepper, salt, sliced onions, and bay leaves: then flour them well, and fry them in clarified butter. When you dish them up, send with them melted butter and anchovy sauce in separate boats. Garnish with fried parsley and slices of lemon.

To fry Lampreys.

Save the blood of your lampreys, wash them in hot water to take off the slime, and cut them into pieces. Fry them (not quite enough) in fresh butter; then drain out all the fat, pour in a little wine, and give your pan a shake; season them with pepper, salt, nutmeg, sweet herbs, and a bay leaf; put in a few capers, a lump of butter rolled in flour, and the blood that was saved; shake the pan several times, and cover the lampreys close. When they are done, take them out, and lay them in your dish; give the sauce a quick boil, squeeze in a little lemon juice, and pour it over the fish. Make use of lemon for garnish.

To fry Oysters.

Make a batter of milk, flour, eggs, mace, and nutmeg; then wash your oysters clean, dip them in the batter roll them in crumbs of bread, and fry them of a light brown in butter or hog's lard. They are a proper garnish for any dish of fish, as well as for many other dishes.

STEWING.

To stew Beef Steaks.

First half broil your beef steaks, then put them into a stewpan, season them with pepper and salt, just cover them with gravy, and put in a piece of butter rolled in flour: let them stew gently half an hour, then add the yolks

yolks of two eggs beat up, ſtir all together for two or three minutes, and diſh up your ſteaks. Garniſh with pickles and ſcraped horſe-raddiſh.

To ſtew a Rump of Beef.

You muſt half roaſt your beef, then put it in a deep pan, with two quarts of water, one quart of red wine, a ſhalot, ſome ſweet herbs, pepper, and ſalt, two or three blades of mace, and a ſpoonful or two of walnut catchup and lemon pickle; let it ſtew over a moderate fire, cloſe covered, for two hours; then take it up and lay it in a deep diſh: ſtrain the gravy, put in half a pint of muſhrooms and an ounce of morels, thicken it with flour and butter, and pour it over the beef. Garniſh with horſeradiſh and beet-root.

To ſtew Ox Palates.

Having waſhed your palates clean, put them into a ſaucepan of cold water, and let them ſtew ſoftly over a ſlow fire till they are tender; then cut them in ſeveral pieces, and diſh them up with artichoke-bottoms and cocks-combs. Garniſh with ſliced lemon, and ſweetbreads fried or ſtrewed.

To ſtew Veal.

Firſt take ſome veal, either raw, boiled or roaſted, and cut it into thick ſlices; then put theſe pieces in a ſtewpan, with juſt water enough to cover them: ſeaſon them with pepper, ſalt, mace, nutmeg, a ſhallot, ſome lemon-peel, ſweet marjoram, and thyme. When they are ſtewed almoſt enough, put into the liquor ſome muſhroom gravy, a little lemon juice, and a glaſs of white wine, and ſtew them a little while longer; then ſtrain off the ſauce, and thicken it with cream, or butter rolled in flour: pour your ſauce into the diſh, and garniſh with fried oyſters, or with ſlices of lemon and bits of broiled bacon.

To ſtew a Neck or Leg of Mutton.

You muſt firſt bone the joint that you are going to ſtew; then put your meat in a ſaucepan, with ſome whole

whole pepper, salt, mace, and nutmeg, one anchovy, a turnip, a few sweet herbs, two onions, a pint of ale, a pint of red wine, two quarts of water, and a hard crust of bread; cover it close, and when it is stewed enough, serve it up with toasts and the gravy.—N. B. An ox-cheek may be dressed in the same manner.

To stew Mutton Chops.

Put them into a shallow tin pan, with a very small quantity of water, and some pepper and salt; cover your pan very close, and place it over a slow fire. When the chops are done (which will be in a very short time) dish them up with their own liquor, and garnish with pickles.

To stew a Pig.

Let your pig be roasted till it is hot through: then skin it, cut it in pieces, and put it in your stewpan, together with some strong gravy, a gill of white wine, an onion, a little marjoram, a piece of butter, three or four spoonfuls of elder vinegar, some salt, pepper, and nutmeg. When it is enough, take it out, laying it upon sippets, and serve it up with sliced lemon for garnish.

To stew a Hare.

Cut the hare into pieces, and lay it in a stew-pan, with a quart of beef gravy, an onion stuck with cloves, an anchovy, some pepper, salt, sweet herbs, &c. Cover it close, and let it stew till it is tender; then put it in a soup dish, and having thickened your gravy with butter and flour, pour it over the hare; lay sippets in the dish, and garnish with slices of lemon.

To stew Rabbits.

Divide your rabbits into quarters, lard them with pretty large slips of bacon, and fry them; then put them in a stew-pan, with a quart of good broth, a glass of white wine, a bunch of sweet herbs, a little pepper and salt, and a piece of butter rolled in flour. When they are enough, dish them up, and pour the sauce on them. Garnish with sliced orange.

To stew a Turkey or Fowl.

Put your fowl or turkey into a saucepan, with a sufficient quantity of gravy, a bunch of celery cut small, an onion, a sprig of thyme, and a muslin rag filled with mace, pepper, cloves, and other spice; let these stew gently till they are enough; then take up your fowl or turkey, thicken the sauce with flour and butter, and pour it in your dish.—N. B. You may stew neck of veal in the same manner.

To stew Ducks or Pidgeons.

First stuff their bellies with a seasoning made of sweet herbs, pepper, salt, cloves, and mace, mixed up with a piece of butter; then set them before the fire, and when they are half roasted, put them in a stew-pan, with a sufficiency of good gravy, a few pickled mushrooms, some white or red wine, a bit of lemon peel, a small bundle of sweet herbs, some whole pepper, mace, and a piece of onion: when they are done, take them out, thicken the sauce with butter and the yolks of eggs, and pour it over your ducks or pidgeons. Garnish with sliced lemon, or with shalots.—N. B. Ducks are frequently stewed with green peafe.

To stew a Goose.

You must cut the goose down the back, bone it, and stuff it with forcemeat; then sew it up, and fry it of a fine brown; after which you must put it into a deep stewpan with two quarts of beef gravy, cover it close, and let it stew for two hours: then take it up and skim off the fat, add to the gravy a glass of red wine, two or three spoonfuls of catchup and lemon pickle, an anchovy shred fine, some beaten mace, pepper, and salt, and a lump of butter rolled in flour; give it a boil, dish up your goose, and strain the sauce over it.

To stew Giblets.

Pick and wash the giblets clean, skin the feet, cut off the bill, split the head in two, break the pinion bones in two, cut the liver and gizzard in quarters, and the

neck

neck in two pieces. Stew them in a proper quantity of water or mutton broth, with a bunch of sweet herbs, a small onion, a spoonful of catchup, one anchovy, two or three cloves, and a few pepper corns; when they are tender, put in the pan a spoonful or two of cream, and a little flour and butter, to thicken the gravy; then lay the giblets in a soup dish, pour the sauce upon them, and garnish with sippets.

To stew Partridges.

Having stuffed your partridges with beaten mace, pepper, salt, and a lump of butter, flour them well, and fry them of a light brown; then put them into a stewpan, with a quart of good gravy, a spoonful or two of Madeira wine and lemon pickle, one anchovy, a few sweet herbs, and half a lemon: when they have stewed half an hour, take them out, thicken the gravy, boil it up, pour it on the partridges, and lay round them artichoke-bottoms boiled and cut in quarters.

To stew a Pheasant.

Take artichoke-bottoms parboiled, and some chesnuts roasted and peeled; stew your pheasant in veal gravy, and when it is enough, put in the chesnuts and artichoke-bottoms, some lemon juice, a little pepper, salt, beaten mace, and a glass of white wine; thicken the sauce with butter and flour, pour it over the pheasant, and lay some forcemeat balls or fried sausages in the dish.

To stew Cod.

When you have cut your cod into slices, put them in a large stewpan, with half a pint of white wine, a pint of gravy, some sweet herbs, an onion, a little salt, mace, pepper, and nutmeg, and likewise a few oysters and their liquor. Let them stew till they are almost enough; then put in a lump of butter rolled in flour, and stew them a little longer. Dish them up with the sauce poured over them, and garnish with lemon.

To

To stew a Trout.

Take a few crumbs of bread, two or three eggs buttered, a piece of lemon-peel, a little thyme, nutmeg, salt and pepper; mix them altogether, and stuff the belly of your trout with them; then put it in a stewpan, with some gravy and white wine, and a lump of butter. When it is done, serve it up with the sauce in the dish, and garnish with lemon cut in slices.

To stew Eels.

After having skinned, gutted, and washed your eels very clean, you must cut them in longish pieces, and put them in your pan, with a little water, a glass of red wine, an onion stuck with cloves, some sweet herbs, mace, salt, and whole pepper; cover the pan close, and let them stew very softly. Before you take them up, put in a piece of butter rolled in flour; and when they are enough, dish them up, and pour the sauce over them.

To stew Carp or Tench.

Scale and gut your carp or tench, wash and dry them, dust them with flour, and fry them of a light brown in dripping or suet: then put them into a stewpan, with a quart of water, a quart of red wine, a spoonful or two of lemon pickle and walnut catchup, an onion stuck with cloves, a piece of horse-radish, some nutmeg, mace, pepper, and salt. When your fish are done, take them out, thicken the gravy with flour and butter, boil it a little, and strain it over your carp or tench. Garnish the dish with pickled mushrooms and scraped horseradish.

To stew Plaice, Soles, or Flounders.

First half fry them in butter, then take them up; add to the butter a quart of water, and boil it slowly a quarter of an hour with a sliced onion and two anchovies; then put in your fish again, and when they have stewed gently for twenty minutes, take them out; thicken the sauce with butter rolled in flour, give it a boil, and strain it through a hair sieve over your fish.

To stew Oysters, Muscles, and all Kinds of Shell Fish.

Having opened your oysters or muscles, put their liquor into a tossing pan, with a little beaten mace, thicken it with butter and flour, and let it boil a few minutes; then put in your shell-fish, with a spoonful or two of cream, and give the pan a shake; serve them up with toasted sippets and the liquor, and garnish them with lemon or crumbs of bread.

HASHING.

To hash Mutton.

Half roast your mutton, and when it is cold, cut it in small pieces; then put a pint of gravy or broth into a tossing-pan, with a spoonful of catchup, a little pepper and salt, and a sliced onion; set this over the fire, thicken it with a piece of butter rolled in flour; and when it boils put in your meat: have ready some toasted sippets, lay them in the dish, and pour your hash on them. Garnish with horse-radish and pickles.

To hash Beef.

Cut the rawest part of a joint of roast beef into very thin slices; then take some gravy and a little water, and boil it with an onion sliced, a bunch of sweet herbs, a spoonful or two of catchup and lemon pickle, some pepper, salt, and grated nutmeg. Then put in your sliced beef, and shake it over the fire till it is quite hot; dish it up with sauce, and garnish with pickled onions or scraped horse-radish.

To mince Veal.

Take any part of veal, either boiled or roasted, that is under-done, and cut it in very small pieces; grate some nutmeg over it, and scatter on it a little flour, salt, and shred lemon peel; then put some gravy in a saucepan, with two or three spoonfuls of catchup, and a lump of butter rolled in flour; when it boils, put in your veal,

with

with a spoonful of cream. Serve it up with sippets in the dish, and garnish with lemon.

To hash Venison.

Let your venison be cut in thin slices; then put into a tossing-pan a spoonful or two of mushroom catchup, a gill of red wine, a little gravy, half an anchovy chopped small, and an onion stuck with cloves; as soon as these boil, put in the venison, and let it boil a few minutes; then pour it with the liquor into a soup-dish, and garnish with red cabbage.

To hash a Calf's Head.

First parboil your calf's head, and when it is cold, cut off the meat in thin slices, and fry it in butter; then put it into a stewpan, with some strong gravy, a glass of red wine, a few sweet herbs, a little lemon-peel, and some spice; toss it up with a lump of butter, and when it is enough, dish it up with the gravy, and garnish with the brains fried, and lemon sliced.

To hash a cold Fowl or Turkey.

You must cut up your fowl or turkey and divide the breast, legs, or wings, &c. into three or four pieces each; then put the several pieces in a stewpan, with a pint of gravy, two or three spoonfuls of lemon pickle and mushroom catchup, a little beaten mace, and a slice of lemon; just before you take them up, put in a spoonful of good cream, and a piece of butter rolled in flour, and shake all together over the fire; then pour the whole into your dish, lay sippets round the bottom, and garnish with lemon or parsley.

To hash Rabbits.

Half roast your rabbits, then take the flesh off the bones, and having minced it small, put it in a stewpan, with some good mutton broth, a little vinegar, a lump of butter, one or two shalots, some shred parsley and grated nutmeg: dish up your hash with sippets, and garnish with sliced lemon.

BAKING.

BAKING.

To bake Mutton Chops.

Cut a neck or loin of mutton into steaks, season them with pepper and salt, butter your baking-dish, and lay them in it; then take a little flour, a quart of milk, six eggs beat up fine, and some ginger, mix it all up together, pour it over your steaks, and send them to the oven: they will be done in an hour and a half.

To bake a Leg of Beef.

Take a leg of beef, cut and hack it, and lay it in a large earthen pan; put to it a bunch of sweet herbs, a piece of carrot, two onions stuck with cloves, a quart of stale beer, some mace, salt, and whole pepper, and cover it with water; fasten to the top of the pan some buttered brown paper, send it to the oven, and let your beef be nicely baked; then strain off the liquor through a coarse sieve; after which you must pick out all the sinews and fat, and put them into a saucepan with a few spoonfuls of the gravy, a little red wine, some mustard, and a piece of butter rolled in flour; shake the saucepan frequently, and when the sauce is thick and hot, pour it over your beef, and serve it up. You may bake an ox's head the same way.

To bake a Calf's Head, or Sheep's Head.

Wash and clean the head well; then take some crumbs of bread, a little shred lemon-peel, a few sweet herbs chopped small, some pepper, salt, and nutmeg; strew these over the head, lay it on an earthen dish, cover it with pieces of butter, and flour it all over; put a little water in the dish, and let the head be baked in a quick oven. When you dish it up, pour over it some strong gravy, with the brains boiled and mixed in it, and garnish your dish with lemon.

To bake a Bullock's Heart.

Stuff it with the same stuffing that I have before directed to be used for a roast fillet of veal, lard it all over with pieces of bacon, skewer it up close to keep in the stuffing, place it in a deep baking dish, and send it to the oven; when baked, lay the heart in another dish, take off the fat, strain the gravy through a sieve, put it in a sauce-pan with a spoonful of red wine and lemon pickle, an anchovy cut small, some beaten mace, and half an ounce of morels, thicken it with butter and flour, pour it on your bullock's heart, and set it to table garnished with barberries.—N. B. When you roast a bullock's or calf's heart, you may stuff it in the same manner, baste it with butter while it is roasting, and serve it up with gravy.

To bake a Pig.

When you have stuffed your pig with chopped sage, pepper, and salt, flour it well, rub it over with butter, and having buttered the dish you lay it in, send it to the oven; when it is baked, put it in a different dish, cut it up, pour over it some gravy, and serve it up.

To bake Fish.

First butter your baking pan, then lay the fish in it, and scatter on them some flour and salt; put a little water in the pan, with two or three onions, a few sweet herbs, and stick bits of butter on your fish. Let them be baked of a fine brown; when they are done, skim off all the fat, and dish them up with what fish-sauce you like.

CHAP. IV.

OF FRICASSEES, RAGOUTS,
And all Sorts of MADE DISHES.

To fricasee Beef.

YOU must cut your beef into small pieces, and fry them in suet with some onions chopped small; then pour off the fat, and put the meat and onions in a stew-a stewpan, with some warm water or broth, a little verjuice or vinegar, a lump of butter, and some pepper and salt; stir it often, and let it stew till it becomes thick. You may put to it some pickled mushrooms, oysters or what other pickles you like, and send it hot to table.

To fricassee Veal.

First parboil your veal, then cut it in square pieces, put it into a saucepan, with a good quantity of strong broth, an onion, and a bunch of sweet herbs, and let it boil for some time; then take a quarter of a pound of butter, two anchovies cut small, and the yolks of three or four eggs, and having tossed all together in a stewpan till it grows thick, put your veal into it. When it is enough, serve it up with mushrooms, either pickled or otherwise, and garnish with lemon sliced.

To fricassee Lamb.

Having cut a hind quarter of lamb into thin slices, season them with spice, sweet herbs, and a shalot; then fry them, and toss them up in a strong gravy, with a little white or red wine, a few oysters, two palates, some forcemeat-balls, a little burnt butter, and two or three eggs: serve all up in one dish, and garnish with lemon.

To fricassee Neat's Tongues.

When you have boiled them tender, you must peel them, cut them in thin slices, and fry them in fresh butter; then pour out the butter, put in some gravy, an onion, some pepper, salt, mace, and sweet herbs, and let them simmer together half an hour; after which, take out the tongues, strain the gravy, put it with the tongues in the stewpan again, with a glass of white wine, some grated nutmeg, a piece of butter rolled in flour, and the yolks of two eggs; shake all together for five or six minutes, and dish up the tongues with the sauce.

A fricassee of Lamb-Stones and Sweetbreads.

Skin your lamb-stones, parboil and slice them, flour your sweetbreads and cut them in slices; season them with

with pepper and falt, dip them in eggs, and fry them in good butter; then ftew them in fome gravy, with a fpoonful or two of white wine, a little lemon-juice, and the yolks of three or four eggs; when they are enough, lay them in your difh, pour the fauce over them, and garnifh with crifped parfley and lemon-peel.

To fricaffee Calves' Feet.

Firft boil the feet, then take out the long bones, cut the meat in thin flices, and put it into a ftewpan, with a little gravy, two or three fpoonfuls of white wine, the yolks of four eggs, a large fpoonful or two of cream, a lump of butter, fome grated nutmeg, and falt; ftir all together till it is enough, then pour the whole into your difh, and garnifh with lemon.

To fricaffee a Pig.

Let your pig be half-roafted; then take off the fkin, pull the meat in flakes from the bones, and put it in a ftewpan, with a little vinegar, fome gravy, white wine, an onion ftuck with cloves, fome lemon-peel, mace, falt, and fweet herbs; when it is nearly done, take out the onion, lemon-peel, and fweet herbs, put in a few mufhrooms, and thicken the gravy with eggs and cream. The head of the pig muft be roafted whole, and placed in the middle of the difh: lay your fricaffee round it, and make ufe of lemon for garnifh.

To fricaffee Rabbits.

Parboil the rabbits, cut them in pieces, flour them and fry them in butter. Meanwhile take the yolks of fix eggs, a pint of ftrong broth, a little white wine, fome chopped parfley and grated nutmeg, a few cockscombs boiled tender, mufhrooms, morels, and artichoke-bottoms; put thefe into a ftewpan with your rabbits, and keep fhaking the pan over the fire till they are done; then difh them on fippets, pour the fauce on them, and garnifh with lemon, parfley, and barberries.—N. B. Chickens may be fricaffeed in the fame manner as rabbits.

Of FRICASSEES.

To fricaſſee Pidgeons.

Cut them in ſmall pieces, and fry them; then ſtew them in ſome good mutton gravy, with a ſpoonful of catchup, a ſlice of lemon, and half an ounce of morels; when they are enough, take them up, thicken the gravy, and ſtrain it over the pidgeons: lay round them forcemeat balls, and garniſh your diſh with pickles.

To fricaſee moſt kinds of Fiſh.

Take a bunch of ſweet herbs, two or three anchovies, an onion ſtuck with cloves, ſome mace, nutmeg, pepper, and lemon-peel; mix theſe ingredients in ſome water or broth, and when they have ſtewed for ſome time, ſtrain off the liquor, and put it in another ſtewpan with melted butter and red or white wine; then, having cut your fiſh in pieces, put them in the pan, and ſoon after put in a few oyſters, capers, pickled muſhrooms, and the yolks of four or five eggs beat up in milk or cream: ſtir the whole together till your fiſh are done enough.

To fricaſſee Eggs.

Let your eggs be boiled hard, then cut them in round ſlices, and put them in a ſtewpan, with half a pint of cream, a glaſs of white wine, and a good piece of butter; ſhake all together over a clear fire, lay your eggs, in a diſh or plate, and pour the ſauce on them: garniſh with toaſted ſippets, and hard eggs cut in two.

To fricaſſee Muſhrooms.

Take a quart of freſh muſhrooms, clean them well, cut them in quarters, put them into a ſaucepan with three or four ſpoonfuls of water, three of milk, and a little ſalt, and let them boil up three times; then add to them half a pint of thick cream, a lump of butter rolled in flour, a little beaten mace and nutmeg, and ſhake the ſauce-pan well. When the liquor is of a proper thickneſs, diſh up your muſhrooms, and pour the ſauce over them.

To ragoo a Leg of Mutton.

First take off all the skin and fat, and cut your meat very thin; then butter your stewpan, throw some flour into it, and put in your mutton, with a few sweet herbs, a blade or two of mace, half a lemon and half an onion, cut very small; stir it two or three minutes, and then put in a quarter of a pint of gravy, and an anchovy shred fine, mixed with flour and butter; stir it again for six or seven minutes, then dish it up, and send it to table.

A Leg or Shoulder of Mutton stuffed.

Take some grated bread, beef-suet, a piece of onion, two or three anchovies, the yolks of hard eggs, a little thyme and savory, a dozen oysters, some salt, pepper, and grated nutmeg; mix all these together, chop them very fine, work them up with raw eggs to the consistence of a paste, stuff your mutton under the skin with them, and then roast it: serve it up with oyster sauce, and garnish with horse raddish.

A Harracoo of Mutton or Lamb.

Cut a neck or loin of mutton or lamb into steaks, flour them, and fry them of a light brown; then pour out all the fat, and put to your meat some turnips and carrots cut in the shape of dice, a little gravy, two or three lettuces chopped small, a bunch of sweet herbs, five or six small onions, some chesnuts peeled, a little salt, pepper, and mace; cover the pan close, and let them stew an hour.

To force a Sirloin of Beef.

Having roasted your sirloin, take it up, and lay it in a dish with the inside uppermost; then with a knife lift up the skin, chop the inside very fine, pour on it a glass of red wine, shake over it some pepper and salt, with two shalots shred fine, then cover it with the skin, and send it up. You may force a rump of beef in the same manner.

To make Beef A-la-mode.

You must cut a buttock of beef into pieces of about two

Of RAGOUTS.

two pounds each, lard them with bacon, and fry them brown; then put them into a pot just large enough to hold them, with two quarts of gravy, a few sweet herbs, an onion, some pepper, salt, cloves, mace, and nutmeg; cover them close, and stew them till they are tender; skim off all the fat, lay your meat in the dish, and strain the sauce over it. You may serve it up either cold or hot.

To make Beef Olives.

Cut some square steaks off a rump of beef, rub them over with the yolk of an egg, strew on them bread-crumbs, grated nutmeg, mace, pepper, and salt, roll them up, skewer them close, and set them before the fire to brown; then put them into a tossing pan, with a pint of gravy, a spoonful or two of lemon pickle and catchup, and a piece of butter rolled in flour: when you dish them up, lay round them forcemeat-balls, the yolks of hard eggs, or mushrooms.

To ragoo a Breast of Veal.

Let your breast of veal be half roasted; then bone it, and put it in a tossing-pan, with a quart of gravy, and an ounce of morels and truffles; stew it till tender, and just before you thicken the gravy, put in a few oysters, mushrooms, and pickled cucumbers cut in small square pieces, with the yolks of four eggs; cut the sweetbread in slices, and fry it of a light brown. When your veal is done, dish it up with sauce, lay the sweetbread round it, and garnish with lemon or pickled barberries.

To make Veal Olives.

Cut your veal into thin slices; then take some marrow, parsley, thyme, marjoram, cloves, mace, salt, pepper and nutmeg; mix these together, and roll them up with your slices, of veal. Fasten your meat on a small spit, baste it with butter, and when it is roasted, serve it up with a sauce made of butter and the juice of a few oranges.

A Ragout of Lamb.

Take a quarter of lamb, cut in four pieces, lard it with flips of bacon, and tofs it up a little in a ftew-pan to brown it; then ftew it in good broth, with falt, pepper, mace, cloves, mufhrooms, and fweet herbs. For fauce, mix up two anchovies and fome fried oyfters with a few fpoonfuls of wine and the juice of half a lemon; lay your lamb in the difh, and pour the fauce over it.

To drefs a Lamb's Head and Pluck.

You muft fkin and fplit the head, wafh it very clean, and lay it in warm water till it looks white; then wafh and clean the pluck, and lay it alfo in water. Boil the head and pluck tender; then mince the heart, liver, and lights very fmall, put them in a toffing-pan with a quart of gravy, half a lemon, a little catchup, pepper, and falt, thicken the gravy with cream, flour, and butter, and juft boil it up. When the head is boiled, rub it over with the yolks of eggs, ftrew on it fome crumbs of bread, chopped parfley, falt, pepper, and grated nutmeg; bafte it well with butter, and brown it before the the fire, or with a falamander. Difh up the head with the heart, liver, and lights; pour your fauce into the difh, and garnifh with lemon or pickles.

To drefs Lamb's Trotters.

Firft boil them, then take out the middle bone, ftuff them with good forcemeat, dip them in eggs, ftrew bread crumbs over them, and fry them brown. Garnifh your difh with crifped parfley.

To ragoo Sweetbreads.

Having cut them in pieces of the fize of a walnut, put them in a ftewpan with hot burnt butter, and ftir them till they are brown; then add to them fome gravy, mufhrooms, pepper, falt, and all-fpice, and let them ftew half an hour. Thicken the gravy, ftrain it through a-fieve, and when you have difhed up your fweetbreads, pour it on them. Garnifh with fliced orange or lemon.

Of RAGOUTS.

To dress Pig's Pettitoes.

Put the pettitoes, and the heart, liver and lights, in a saucepan, with half a pint of water, an onion, a bunch of sweet herbs, some whole pepper and a blade of mace; when they have boiled eight or ten minutes, take out the liver, lights, and heart, mince them very fine, and scatter on them flour and grated nutmeg; let the feet boil till they are tender, then take them out and split them; strain the liquor, thicken it with flour and butter, put in the pettitoes and mincemeat, and shake the saucepan a little over the fire. Lay sippets round the dish, pour in your mincemeat, and lay the feet over it.

To ragoo Pig's Feet and Ears.

Boil the feet and ears tender, then split the feet down the middle, cut the ears in narrow pieces, dip them in batter, and fry them of a good brown; after which put a little beef gravy in a stewpan, with a spoonful or two of lemon-pickle and mushroom-catchup, a lump of butter rolled in flour, some mustard, and some salt; put in the feet and ears, give them a boil up, and then lay the feet in the middle of your dish, with the ears round them; strain your sauce, pour it in the dish, and garnish with crisped parsley.

A Ragoo of Venison.

Lard your venison with large pieces of bacon, season it with pepper and salt, and fry it in hog's lard; then stew it three hours in broth or boiling water, with a little white wine, a piece of lemon, some nutmeg, salt, and sweet herbs; thicken the sauce with flour and butter, and pour it in your dish over the venison.

A savory Dish of Lamb's Bits.

When you have skinned and split the stones, you must lay them on a dry cloth with the livers and sweetbreads, flour them all well, and fry them in hot butter or lard; dish them up in melted butter and fried parsley.

To jug a Hare.

You muſt cut your hare in pieces, ſeaſon it with pepper and ſalt, and put it into an earthen jug or pitcher, with a blade or two of mace, a few ſweet herbs, and an onion ſtuck with cloves; cover the jug cloſe, ſet it over the fire, in a pot of boiling water, and let your meat ſtew upwards of three hours; then turn it out into a diſh, and ſend it up with gravy. Garniſh with lemon.

An excellent Method of Dreſſing a Wild Duck.

Half-roaſt your duck, then lay it in a diſh, and carve it, but let the joints be left hanging together; ſeaſon it with ſalt and pepper, ſqueeze over it the juice of a lemon, turn it on the breaſt, and preſs it hard with a plate; add ſome gravy to it, cover it cloſe with another diſh, and ſet it over a ſtove for ten minutes; then ſerve it up, with ſliced lemon for garniſh.

To force Chickens.

When your chickens are roaſted, ſlit the ſkin, cut the meat from the bones, chop it ſmall with parſley and bread crumbs, and mix it up with a little cream, pepper and ſalt; then put in the meat and cloſe the ſkin. Brown the chickens with a ſalamander, and ſend them to table with white ſauce.

Pidgeons in a Hole.

Seaſon your pidgeons with ſalt, pepper, and beaten mace, put into their bellies a ſmall piece of butter, lay them in a diſh, pour over them a little batter, and ſend them to the oven to bake.

To jug Pidgoons.

Pluck and draw them, ſtuff them with a mixture of ſuet, bread-crumbs, the livers chopped, parſley, and the yolks of two eggs; rub them over with pepper and ſalt, and put them in your jug with a good deal of butter; ſtop up the jug cloſe, and ſet it in a kettle of boiling water. When the pidgeons have ſtewed two hours, take them out, and lay them in your diſh; then take the

Of RAGOUTS. 57

the gravy that came from them, add to it a glafs of white wine, a flice of lemon, a fpoonful of cream, a few muſhrooms, and an anchovy ſhred ſmall; thicken it with flour, boil it up, and ſtrain it over your pidgeons. Garniſh the diſh with lemon, or with parſley and red cabbage.

A Ragout of Snipes and Woodcocks.

Cut them down the back, and put them in a ſtew-pan, with ſome good gravy, two or three ſpoonfuls of red wine, a few ſmall muſhrooms, ſome beaten mace, pepper and ſalt, and a piece of butter rolled in flour: when they are done, diſh them up with ſippets, and garniſh with ſliced orange or lemon.

To roaſt or bake a Cod's Head.

Clean the head well, ſtrew on it a little ſalt, pepper, nutmeg, a few crumbs of bread, and ſweet herbs; rub it with butter and eggs, flour it, and ſet it in a pan before the fire to roaſt; or place it in a baking-diſh, with a little broth, vinegar, white wine, and anchovies, and ſend it to the oven to bake. Diſh it up with ſhrimp, lobſter, anchovy, oyſter, or muſcle ſauce, and garniſh with ſmall fiſh fried, ſcraped horſe-raddiſh, and ſliced lemon.

To dreſs a Turtle.

Obſerve to take your turtle out of the water the night before you intend to dreſs it, cut off the head, and ſave the blood; then with a ſharp knife ſeparate the callipee (the belly) from the callipaſh (the back) down to the ſhoulders, take out the entrails, and throw them into a tub of water, taking particular care not to burſt the gall, but to cut it from the liver, and throw it away; then ſeparate each diſtinctly, and having put the guts in another veſſel, ſplit them open with a penknife, draw them through a woollen cloth in warm water, to clear away the ſlime, and then put them in clean cold water, with the other part of the entrails, which muſt be all cut in ſmall pieces. Meanwhile diſunite the back and

belly

belly entirely, and cut off the fins, which you muſt ſcald and cut ſmall, and lay them by themſelves ready to be ſeaſoned; then cut off the meat from the belly and back in middling pieces, lay it likewiſe by itſelf; after which ſcald the back and belly, pull the ſhell off the back, and the yellow ſkin from the belly, and with a cleaver cut thoſe up into pieces, about the ſize of a card; put theſe pieces in cold water, waſh them out, and lay them by themſelves on the dreſſer. The meat being thus parted and prepared for ſeaſoning, mix a proper quantity of ſalt with ſome Cayenne pepper, beaten mace, and nutmeg; the quantity of each being proportioned to the ſize of your turtle, ſo that in each diſh there may be three or four ſpoonfuls of ſeaſoning to every twelve pounds of meat. Having ſeaſoned your meat, and provided ſome deep diſhes to bake it in, lay the coarſeſt parts of the meat, with about a quarter of a pound of butter, at the bottom of each diſh, and then ſome of each of the parcels of meat, ſo that all the diſhes may have equal portions of the different parts of the turtle; and between each layer of meat, ſtrew a few ſweet herbs ſhred fine. Let your diſhes be filled within two inches of the top; put into them the blood of the turtle boiled; then lay on forcemeat balls, highly ſeaſoned; put in each diſh a ſufficiency of water, and a gill of Madeira wine; then break over them five or ſix eggs, to prevent the meat from being ſcorched at the top, and over theſe ſcatter a little parſley. This done, put your diſhes into a hot oven, and in an hour and an half, or two hours (according to the ſize of the diſhes) your meat will be enough.

To dreſs Mock Turtle.

You muſt take a large calf's head with the ſkin on it, and ſcald off the hair; then clean it well, cut it in thin ſlices, and put it into a ſtewpan, with the brains, a quart of ſtrong gravy, a pint of Madeira wine, a tea-ſpoonful of Cayenne pepper, a little ſalt, half the peel of a large lemon ſhred very fine, a few chopped oyſters, the juice of three or four lemons, and ſome ſweet herbs cut ſmall;

Of RAGOUTS.

small; stew all these together till your meat is very tender, which will be in about an hour and a half. In the mean time have ready the back shell of a turtle, lined with a paste of flour and water, which you must first harden in an oven; put your meat in the shell together with the ingredients, and set in the oven to brown the top; that being done garnish the top with forcemeat balls and the yolks of hard eggs, and serve it up.—N. B. If you cannot easily procure the shell of a turtle, a china soup dish will answer the same purpose.

A Ragout of Sturgeon.

First cut your sturgeon into slices, then lard those slices, rub them over with the yolk of an egg, flour them a little, and fry them brown with hog's lard; after which put them in a stewpan, with some gravy, sweet herbs, a glass of white wine, slices of lemon, truffles, mushrooms, and veal sweetbreads cut in pieces. Garnish your dish with lemon and barberries.

To ragoo Cucumbers.

Pare your cucumbers, cut them in slices, and fry them in fresh butter; then drain them in a sieve, and put them into a stewpan, with a little gravy, a glass of red or white wine, and a blade or two of mace: when they have stewed six or seven minutes, put in a piece of butter rolled in flour, shake the pan over the fire, and when the sauce is thick dish up your cucumbers.

To stew Green Pease with Lettuces.

Boil your pease in spring water with a little salt in it; then take two or three lettuces, slice them, and fry them with good butter; after that put your pease and lettuces in a stewpan, with some nice gravy, a little shred mint, pepper and salt; thicken with butter and flour, and when they are done serve them up in a soup dish.

Forcemeat Balls for Made Dishes.

Mince half a pound of veal, with the same quantity of suet, take a few sweet herbs shred fine, some beaten mace

mace and nutmeg, a little lemon peel cut small, the yolks of two or three eggs, some pepper and some salt; mix all these ingredients well together, make them up into little balls, roll them in flour, and fry them brown. They are a great addition to most made dishes.

A Ragout for made Dishes.

Take some lamb stones and cocks-combs boiled, blanched, and sliced; toss them up in a stewpan, with gravy, red or white wine, sliced sweetbreads, mushrooms, oysters, morels, truffles, sweet herbs, and spice; thicken the whole with burnt butter, and make use of it to enrich any kind of ragout.

CHAP. V.

Of SOUPS, BROTHS, GRAVIES, and SAUCES.

To make Pease Soup.

TO a quart of split pease put a gallon of water, with a bunch of sweet herbs, two or three onions, some whole pepper, a pound of mutton, and a pound of lean beef; boil them together, till the meat is quite tender, and the soup strong; then strain it through a sieve, and pour it into a clean saucepan; put to it three or four heads of celery washed clean and cut small, some spinach and dried mint, and let it boil a little while longer; then pour it in your soup dish, and serve it up with bread cut in dice and fried brown.

To make Gravy Soup.

Boil the bones of a rump of beef, and a piece of the neck; then strain off the liquor, and put it in a saucepan with a lump of butter, some celery, spinach, endive, a piece of carrot, an onion stuck with cloves, some mace, salt, and pepper: boil all these together, and dish up your soup with a French roll sliced and toasted.

Of SOUPS.

To make Green Peaſe Soup.

Take a ſmall knuckle of veal, and a pint and a half of old green peaſe; put them in a ſaucepan with five or ſix quarts of water, a few blades of mace, a ſmall onion ſtuck with cloves, ſome ſweet herbs, ſalt, and whole pepper; cover them cloſe, and boil them; then ſtrain the liquor through a ſieve, and put it in a freſh ſaucepan, with a pint of young peaſe, a lettuce, the heart of a cabbage, and three or four heads of celery, cut ſmall; cover the pan, and let them ſtew an hour. Pour the ſoup into your diſh, and ſerve it up with the cruſt of a French roll.

To make Onion Soup.

Firſt put half a pound of butter into a ſtewpan, and boil it till it has ceaſed to make a noiſe; then take ten or twelve onions peeled and cut ſmall, flour them, throw them into the butter, and fry them about a quarter of an hour; after which pour in your pan three pints of boiling water, ſtir it round, and put in a cruſt of bread. Seaſon the liquor with pepper and ſalt according to your palate, ſtir it frequently, and let it boil ten minutes; then take it off the fire, beat up the yolks of two eggs with a ſpoonful of vinegar, mix them well with your ſoup, and ſerve it up.

To make Barley Soup.

Take four quarts of water, half a pound of barley, a cruſt of bread, ſome lemon-peel, and a blade or two of mace: boil them till the liquor is half waſted; then add half a pint of white wine, and ſweeten the ſoup to your taſte.

An excellent White Soup.

Take a knuckle of veal, a pound of lean bacon, and a fowl, put them in a large ſaucepan with ſix quarts of water, half a pound of rice, a few ſweet herbs, one or two onions, ſome whole pepper, two anchovies, and ſome celery; boil all together till the ſoup is ſufficiently

F ſtrong,

strong, strain it through a sieve into a clean earthen vessel, and let it stand all night; then skim it well, and pour it into a tossing pan, with half a pound of Jordan almonds beat fine, the yolks of one or two eggs, and a pint of cream: boil it up, strain it, and send it to table hot.

To make a Pocket or Portable Soup.

Strip all the skin and fat off a leg of veal, and part the flesh from the bones; boil this flesh in three or four gallons of soft water, till the liquor becomes a strong jelly, and the meat has lost its virtue; then strain the jelly into an earthen pan, and when it is cold, skim off the fat from the top. Put a large stewpan of boiling water over a stove, and filling some deep cups with the jelly, set them in your stewpan. Take great care that the water do not run over into the cups, for if it does, it will spoil your jelly. Let the water boil softly till the jelly is as thick as glue; then take out the cups, and when they are cool, turn out the jelly into a piece of new flannel, which will gradually draw out all the moisture, and let it lie in the flannel till it is perfectly dry. Keep these cakes in a dry place, and they will presently become so hard, that you may carry them in your pocket without the least inconvenience. When you make use of it, take a piece about the size of a large walnut, and pour a pint of boiling water on it; stir it till it is melted, and season it to your palate.— N. B. It will keep good for many months.

To make Eel Soup.

To every pound of eels put a quart of water, an onion, a blade or two of mace, a crust of bread, a bunch of sweet herbs, and some whole pepper: cover them close, and boil them till half the liquor is wasted; then strain it, lay some toasted bread in the dish, and pour in your soup.

To make strong Gravy.

You must take part of a leg of beef, and the scrag end of a neck of mutton, break the bones, and put your meat

Of GRAVIES.

meat in a saucepan, with a sufficient quantity of water; when it boils, put in a few sweet herbs, an onion stuck with cloves, some salt, pepper, and nutmeg: boil your meat till its strength is drawn out, then strain off the liquor, and keep it for use.

To draw Beef, Mutton, or Veal Gravy.

Take a pound of either beef, mutton or veal, cut it in thin slices, lay a piece of bacon at the bottom of your saucepan or stewpan, and place the meat on it; put in some slices of carrot, and cover the pan close for a few minutes; then pour in a quart of boiling water, with some spice, an onion, sweet herbs, and a piece of toasted bread. Thicken the gravy with flour and butter, season it with salt, and when it is good to your liking, strain it off. The bacon may be omitted if you dislike it.

To make White Gravy.

Cut a pound of veal into small pieces, and boil it in a quart of water, with an onion, two or three cloves, a few pepper-corns, some sweet herbs, and a blade or two of mace: when the liquor is of a proper strength, strain it off.

To make a strong Fish Gravy.

You must cut two or three small fish of any kind into little pieces, and put them into a saucepan of water, with some sweet herbs, lemon-peel, mace, whole pepper, and a crust of bread toasted: when these have boiled some time, put in a piece of butter and flour, and let them boil a little while longer; then strain off the liquor for use.

A good Gravy for any Use.

First take two ounces of butter, and brown it in a stewpan; then put in two pounds of gravy beef, two quarts of water, and half a pint of red or white wine, with two or three shalots, five or six mushrooms, four anchovies, some whole pepper, mace, and cloves: let these

these stew an hour over a moderate fire, then strain off your gravy.

To make Mutton Broth.

Having cut a neck of mutton in two, boil the scrag end in a gallon of water, with a bunch of sweet herbs, a crust of bread, and an onion; when it has boiled an hour, put in the other part of the mutton, and about ten minutes before your broth is enough, put in some turnips, dried marigolds, a little shred parsley, and a few chives chopped small.

To make Beef Broth.

First crack the bone of a leg of beef in two or three parts; then put the beef into a pot, with four quarts of water, a crust of bread, some mace, salt, and parsley. When the meat and sinews are quite tender, cut some toasted bread into square pieces, lay the bread in your soup dish, put in your meat, and pour the liquor over it.

To make Chicken Broth.

Having skinned a chicken, you must split it in two, and boil it in as much water as you think sufficient with a crust of bread, and a blade or two of mace; let it boil gently till the broth is good, then strain it off.

To make a standing Sauce.

Put a quart of red or white wine in a glazed jar; then take four or five anchovies, six shalots, the juice of two lemons, some whole pepper, mace, cloves, ginger, lemon-peel, horse-radish, sweet herbs, two spoonfuls of capers and their liquor; put all these in a linen bag, then put the bag into the jar with the wine, stop the jar close, set it for an hour in a kettle of boiling water, and keep it for use in a warm place. A spoonful or two of this liquor may be put into any sauce.

To melt Butter.

When you melt butter, you must take care that your saucepan be well tinned and very clean; moisten the bottom with a spoonful of water, dust your butter with flour,

Of SAUCES.

flour, cut it in flices, and put it into the faucepan. As it melts, you muſt frequently ſhake your faucepan one way, that the butter may not turn to oil; and when it is entirely melted, give it a boil up.

To make Sauce for roaſted Meat.

Waſh an anchovy very clean, and put it in a ſtewpan, with a little ſtrong broth, a glaſs of red wine, a ſliced ſhalot, the juice of a Seville orange, and ſome grated nutmeg; ſtew theſe together a little while, and then pour the ſauce to the gravy that runs from your meat.

To make Onion Sauce.

Peel your onions, and boil them tender; then throw them into a colander to drain, and having chopped them on a board, put them into a clean faucepan, with a good piece of butter, a gill of cream, and a little falt; ſtir all together over the fire, and when the butter is melted, your ſauce will be done enough.

To make Mint Sauce.

Pick and waſh your mint, chop it ſmall, and put it in a ſmall baſon; then pour in a ſufficient quantity of vinegar mixed with ſugar.

Egg Sauce.

Boil your eggs hard, chop them, put them into ſome good melted butter, and juſt boil them up.

White Sauce for Fowls or Chickens.

Put ſome veal gravy in a ſaucepan, with a ſpoonful of lemon-pickle, one anchovy, and a few pickled muſh-rooms; give it a gentle boil, then put in the yolks of two eggs beat fine, and a little cream; ſhake the pan over the fire, and then ſerve up your ſauce.

Muſhroom Sauce.

Take a pint of muſhrooms, waſh them clean, and put them into your ſaucepan, with a pint of cream, a good lump of butter rolled in flour, ſome mace, nut-meg,

meg, and salt; boil all these together, and continue stirring them till the sauce is thick.

Shalot Sauce.

Peel five or six shalots, cut them small, put to them two or three spoonfuls of water, two of white wine, and two of vinegar; boil them up, and season them with salt and pepper.

Celery Sauce.

Cut your celery into thin bits, and boil it in gravy till it is tender; then add some grated nutmeg, mace, pepper and salt, with a piece of butter rolled in flour, and give it a boil. This sauce is used with roasted or boiled fowls, turkeys, partridges, &c.

To make Apple Sauce.

Pare, core, and slice your apples, put them into a saucepan with a little water and a few cloves, and let them simmer over a slow fire till they are quite soft; then strain off all the water, and beat them up with some butter and brown sugar.

Lemon Sauce for a boiled Fowl.

Take a lemon, peel it, cut it small, and take out all the kernels; bruise the liver of your fowl with three or four spoonfuls of good gravy, then melt some butter, mix all together, give them a gentle boil, and add to the sauce a little shred lemon-peel.

Bread Sauce.

Put a thick piece of stale bread into a pint of water, with a few pepper corns, a bit of onion, and a blade of mace; let it boil till the bread is soft; then take out the spice and onion, pour the water off, and beat the bread well with a spoon; put in a lump of butter and some salt, stir the whole together, and set it on the fire for two or three minutes; then pour it into your sauce boat.

Anchovy.

Of SAUCES.

Anchovy Sauce.

Take an anchovy, and put it into a saucepan, with half a pint of gravy, a glass of red wine, a spoonful of catchup, and a quarter of a pound of butter rolled in flour; boil all together till your sauce is of a proper thickness.

Shrimp Sauce.

Take half a pint of shrimps, pick them clean, and put them into half a pint of gravy; boil it up with a good piece of butter rolled in flour, and a spoonful or two of red wine.

To make Lobster Sauce.

Cut the flesh of a lobster in very small pieces, and mix it with some thick melted butter; boil the whole up together, and season it with a little mace, salt, and pepper.

Oyster Sauce.

Put half a pint of large oysters into a saucepan, with their own liquor, two or three blades of mace, some whole pepper, and a piece of lemon-peel; simmer all together till the oysters are plump, then take them out with a fork, and let the liquor boil five or six minutes; then strain it off, wash out the saucepan clean, and put in the oysters and liquor again, with half a pint of gravy, a spoonful or two of white wine, and half a pound of butter rolled in a little flour; set your pan over the fire, shake it frequently, and let the sauce boil up.

Muscle or Cockle Sauce.

When you have opened your muscles or cockles, put them with their liquor into a stewpan, with a good lump of butter, a glass of white wine, some mace, salt, and pepper, and boil the whole up together.

A very good Sauce for most kinds of Fish.

Take some veal or mutton gravy, mix with it a little of the water that drains from your fish, and put it in a sauce-a faucepan, with a fpoonful of catchup, a glafs of white wine, one anchovy, and an onion: thicken it with a fpoonful of cream, and a lump of butter rolled in flour.

CHAP. VI.

Of PUDDINGS.

General Directions with regard to Puddings.

WHEN you boil puddings, take great care that your bag or cloth be very clean, dip it in hot water, and flour it well. You muft always let the water boil before you put in the pudding; and you fhould frequently move your pudding in the pot, to prevent it from fticking. When your pudding is boiled, juft dip it in a pan of clean cold water, then untie the cloth, and the pudding will turn out without fticking to the cloth. In all baked puddings, you muft butter the pan or difh before your pudding is poured in.

To make a Bread Pudding.

Having cut the crumb of a penny loaf into thin flices, pour over it a quart of boiling milk, cover it up clofe, and let it ftand fome hours to foak; then beat it well with fome melted butter, the yolks and whites of a few eggs, a little falt, and fome grated nutmeg; tie your pudding loofe in the cloth, and let it boil about three quarters of an hour: when it is done, lay it in your difh, and pour on it melted butter and fugar. You may, if you pleafe, put fome currants in your pudding before you boil it.

A Baked Bread Pudding.

You muft put a quarter of a pound of butter into a pint of milk or cream, fet it over the fire, and ftir it well; as foon as the butter is melted, add to the milk a fufficiency of crumbled bread, three or four eggs, half a pound a pound of currants picked and waſhed clean, a good deal of ſugar, ſome grated nutmeg, ginger, and a little ſalt; mix all up together, pour it in a buttered diſh, and ſend it to the oven.

To make a plain boiled Pudding.

Mix with a pint of new milk ſix eggs well beaten, two or three ſpoonfuls of flour, ſome ſugar, a little grated nutmeg and ſalt; put this mixture into a bag or cloth, then put it in your pot, and when it has boiled an hour, ſerve it up with melted butter over it.

A Batter Pudding.

Take a quart of milk, five or ſix ſpoonfuls of flour, ſix eggs, a little ſalt and beaten ginger; mix the whole up together, boil it an hour, and ſend it to table with melted butter and ſugar.

A Rice Pudding.

Put half a pound of rice (either ground or otherwiſe) into three pints of milk, and boil it well; when it is almoſt cold, mix with it ſeven or eight beaten eggs, half a pound of butter, ſome cinnamon, mace, and nutmeg, and half a pound of ſugar: you may either boil or bake it.

A Marrow Pudding.

Slice a penny loaf into a quart of boiling cream or milk; add to it a pound of beef marrow ſhred fine, the yolks of eight eggs, three ſpoonfuls of roſe water, a glaſs of brandy or ſack, a quarter of a pound of currants, ſome candied citron and lemon ſliced thin, grated nutmeg, and ſugar; mix all together, and either boil it, or ſend it to the oven to bake. Stick pieces of citron all over the top of your pudding when you ſerve it up.

To make a plain baked Pudding.

Take a quart of milk, and boil it with a little flour; then put to it ſix ounces of ſugar, half a pound of butter, eight or ten eggs (but not all the whites) ſome ſalt and nutmeg; let the whole be well mixed together, and

and put into your dish; it will be baked enough in little more than half an hour.

A Plumb Pudding.

Mix a quart of milk with a pound of suet cut small, add to it a pound of currants, half a nutmeg grated, a pound of raisins stoned, eight yolks of eggs and four whites, a spoonful of brandy, a little salt, beaten ginger, and some sugar; mix these up well with fine flour, and let your pudding boil hours; or you may send it to the oven to bake. When you boil it let it be dished up with melted butter.

A Custard Pudding.

Take the yolks of six eggs well beaten, two spoonfuls of flour, some sugar and grated nutmeg; mix all together in a pint of new milk or cream, and boil it half an hour; when you serve it up, pour in the dish some melted butter mixed with a little white wine. Baked custard pudding is equally good.

An Apple Pudding.

First make a good puff-paste, and roll it out to the thickness of half an inch, then pare and slice as many apples as will fill the crust, and having closed it up, tie it in a cloth and boil it. If it is a large pudding, it will take three or four hours boiling; if a small one, two hours: when it is done, lay it in a dish, cut a piece of the crust out of the top, and put in butter and sugar to your palate; then lay the crust on again, and serve up your pudding.

N. B. A pear pudding may be made in the same manner, as may likewise puddings of any sort of plumbs, cherries, rasberries, red currants, mulberries, gooseberries, apricots, &c.

To make a baked Apple Pudding.

You must boil your apples tender, and bruise them through a sieve; add to them a quarter of a pound of butter, the yolks of eight eggs, a pound of loaf sugar, a pint

pint of cream, some lemon-juice, and grated nutmeg; mix all together, put a thin puff-paste on the bottom and rims of your dish, pour the pudding in, and let it be baked in a slack oven.

A Lemon Pudding.

First grate the rinds of four lemons; then grate two Naples biscuits, and mix them with your lemon peel; add three quarters of a pound of white sugar, the like quantity of melted butter, twelve yolks of eggs and six whites, the juice of two or three lemons, and half a pint of cream or milk; beat the whole up together, lay a thin crust all over your dish, and having put in your pudding, send it to the oven to bake. An orange pudding may be made the same way.

A Steak Pudding.

Take a quartern of flour and two pounds of suet chopped fine, and mix it up with cold water into a good paste; then season your steaks (which may be either mutton or beef) with pepper and salt; lay them in the crust, and close it up: tie your pudding in a cloth, and put it into the pot. A large steak pudding takes four or five hours boiling; a small one will be done in three hours.

To make a Tansey Pudding.

To a pint of cream put ten eggs well beaten, and some grated bread; season it with nutmeg, some sugar, and a little salt, green it well with the juice of tansey and spinach, mix it up together, put it in a stewpan with a lump of butter, set it over a slow fire, and when it is of a proper thickness, put it in a buttered dish, and bake it. Lay sweetmeats over it when you serve it up.

A Suet Pudding.

Take a pound of suet shred small, a quart of milk, four or five eggs, some flour, a spoonful or two of salt and grated ginger; mix these well together, and let it boil two hours; send it to table with melted butter poured on it.

A Sweet-

A Sweetmeat Pudding.

Lay a thin paste all over your dish, and cover the bottom with candied orange, citron, and lemon peel sliced thin; then beat up the yolks of eight eggs with half a pound of melted butter, and seven or eight ounces of sugar; pour this mixture on your sweetmeats, and bake it in a slack oven.

An Almond Pudding.

You must beat a pound of sweet almonds very fine, with a gill of sack, and three or four spoonfuls of rose water; add near a half a pound of sugar, a quart of cream, the yolks of eight eggs and the whites of four, half a pound of butter melted, two spoonfuls of flour and bread crumbs, some grated nutmeg and cinnamon; mix all well together, and either boil or bake it.

CHAP. VII.

Of PIES, TARTS, &c.

To make Puff Paste.

TAKE a quartern of flour, mix with it half a pound of butter, and make it up into a light paste with water; then roll out your paste, stick pieces of butter all over it, and dust it with a little flour; fold it up, then roll it out again; after this put in more butter, flour it, fold it up, and roll it out: repeat this till your paste is of a proper consistence.

A Paste for Tarts.

Of flour, butter, and sugar, take half a pound each; mix them up together, beat it well with a rolling-pin, and roll it out thin.

A Paste for raised Pies.

You must boil six pounds of butter in a gallon of water, and when it is melted skim it off into a peck of flour; work it up into a paste, pull it in lumps till it is cold, and make it up in whatever form you please. This is a very good crust for a goose pie.

An excellent Paste for Patty-pans.

Take three or four eggs, half a pound of butter, a pound of flour, and two ounces of fine sugar; work it all up into a paste.

A Paste for Custards.

Mix half a pound of flour with three or four spoonfuls of cream, six ounces of butter, and the yolks of two eggs; when mixed, let it stand a quarter of an hour, then work it up well, and roll it out thin.

To make a Steak Pie.

Take some fine rump steaks, or mutton chops, beat them with a rolling pin, and season them with salt and pepper; lay a good puff paste in your dish, put in the steaks, pour some water over them, lay a piece of butter on each steak, put the crust on the top, and send your pie to the oven.

A savory Lamb or Veal Pie.

Cut your veal or lamb into thin slices, and season it with beaten mace, nutmeg, cloves, salt, pepper, and chopped sweet herbs; lay it in your crust; put slices of bacon at the bottom, stick pieces of butter on your meat, and close up your pie. When it is baked, open the pie, and pour in the sauce which I have directed in the following receipt.

A Lear for Savory Pies.

Take some gravy, a gill of red wine, a little oyster liquor, an onion, one or two anchovies, and a bunch of sweet herbs; boil this mixture up, thicken it with burnt butter, and when your pies are baked, pour it into them.

A Savory Chicken Pie.

Season your chickens with salt, mace, and pepper, put

put a piece of butter into each of them, and lay them in your cruſt, with thin ſlices of bacon over them; then put in a pint of good gravy, ſome yolks of hard eggs chopped ſmall, and a few forcemeat balls; cloſe up the pie, and let it be baked in a gentle oven.

A Pigeon Pie.

Stuff the bellies of your pigeons with a lump of butter, ſeaſon them with ſalt and pepper, and lay them in your puff-paſte, together with their gizzards, necks, livers, hearts and pinions, and likewiſe a beef ſteak; put to them as much water as will almoſt fill the diſh, lay on the top cruſt, and ſend your pie to the oven.

To make a Gooſe Pie.

Firſt parboil your gooſe, then bone it, ſeaſon it with ſavory ſpice, lay it in a deep cruſt with a good deal of butter, and let it be well baked. A ſlice of this pie, when cold, makes a pretty little ſide-diſh for ſupper.

A Hare Pie.

Bone your hare, cut it in pieces, and ſeaſon it with pepper, ſalt, nutmeg, and mace; then put it in your pie cruſt, with ſlices of bacon both under and over; when it is baked pour ſome melted butter in your pie.

A Giblet Pie.

Having well cleanſed the giblets, put them into a ſaucepan, with water enough to cover them, ſome whole pepper, mace, ſalt, ſweet herbs, and an onion; cover them cloſe, and let them ſtew gently till they are tender; have ready a good puff-paſte in your diſh, lay a rump ſteak at the bottom, and put in your giblets; then ſtrain the liquor in which they were ſtewed, pour it over them, cloſe up the pie, and ſend it to the oven.

A Veniſon Paſty.

Firſt raiſe a high round pie, then chop a pound of ſuet, and lay it in the bottom; bone your veniſon, cut it in middling pieces, ſeaſon it with ſalt, mace, and pepper, place it on the ſuet, put ſome butter over it, and cloſe up the paſty: when it is baked, fill it up with liquor made from the bones of the veniſon.

To make an Eel Pie.

Cut your eels in pieces of the length of two inches, and season them with pepper, salt, and dried sage; lay a good crust in your dish, put in the eels, and pour a good deal of water over them; close your pie, and let it be well baked.

A Lobster Pie.

Having boiled two or three lobsters, take out all the meat, and cut it in pieces; season it with mace, pepper, and salt, and lay it in your crust; then put in some crumbs of bread mixed up with melted butter, cover the pie with the top crust, and let it be baked in a slow oven. Lobster pie is a good corner dish for a dinner.

A Tench Pie.

Lay a good puff-paste in your dish, put on it a layer of butter, grate over it some nutmeg, mace, cinnamon, pepper, and salt; then put in half a dozen tench, lay some more butter and spice on them, and add to them a gill of claret; close your pie, and bake it: when it comes out of the oven, pour in a little gravy and melted butter.

A Lear for Fish Pies.

Take some oyster liquor, red or white wine, an anchovy or two, a little vinegar, and some melted butter; mix all together, and when your fish pies are baked, pour it in with a funnel.

To make minced Pies.

Having parboiled a tender piece of lean beef, chop it very small; add to it three pounds of suet shred fine, two pounds of currants well picked, washed, and dried at the fire, a pound and a half of raisins stoned and chopped fine, twenty or thirty pippins cut small, a pound of fine sugar, two nutmegs grated, and a proper quantity of mace, cloves, and cinnamon; put all these ingredients into a large pan, pour in half a pint of sack and half a pint of brandy, and mix the whole well together; then put it down clofe in a ftone pot, and it will keep good three or four months. When you make your pies, lay a thin cruft all over your difh or patty-pan, put in a thin layer of the mince-meat, and then a thin layer of candied citron cut fmall, then another layer of mince-meat, and after that a layer of candied orange-peel cut thin, then a little mince-meat; fqueeze in the juice of a Seville orange or lemon, pour in a glafs of red wine, lay on your top cruft, and let the pie be nicely baked. Mince pies eat very well when they are cold.

To make an Apple or Pear Pie.

Pare, core and quarter your apples or pears, lay them in your cruft, and put to them a fufficient quantity of fugar, a little fhred lemon-peel, a few cloves, and fome lemon juice; clofe up your pie, and fend it to the oven. When it is baked, you may put in fome butter; or elfe beat up the yolks of two eggs with half a pint of cream, fweeten it with fugar, and pour it into the pie.

A Goofeberry, Plumb, or Cherry Pie.

Lay a good cruft in your difh, fcatter a little fugar on the bottom, then put in your fruit, and lay fugar over it; put on the upper cruft, and bake your pie in a moderate oven. You may make a red currant pie the fame way.

To make Iceing for Tarts.

Having beat and fifted a quarter of a pound of double refined fugar, put it into a morter, with two fpoonfuls of rofe water, and the white of one egg; beat them all together for half an hour, and then lay it on your tarts with a feather.

To make Tarts of various Kinds.

When you defign to make your tarts in tin pattypans, firft butter the pans, and then lay a thin rich cruft all over them; but when you make them in glafs or china difhes, you need not put any cruft except the upper one; fcatter fine fugar on the bottom, then put in your fruit, and ftrew fugar over it. Let your tarts be baked in a flack oven.

CHAP.

CHAP VIII.

Of CAKES, &c.

To make a good Seed Cake.

TAKE a quartern of flour, two pounds of butter beaten to a cream, a pound and an half of fine sugar, ten yolks of eggs and five whites, some beaten mace, cloves, nutmeg, and cinnamon, three or four ounces of carraway seeds, half a pint of cream, two or three ounces of candied citron and orange-peel, a little new yest, and a spoonful or two of rose water; mix the whole well together, and put it in a tin hoop, which must be papered at the bottom, and buttered: it will take an hour and a half, or two hours in a quick oven. When it is baked, you may ice it over with sugar and the whites of eggs, and then set it again in the oven to harden.

A Pound Cake.

You must beat a pound of butter till it is like fine thick cream, then mix with it twelve yolks of eggs and six whites, a pound of flour, a few carraways, and a pound of sugar: beat it all well together for an hour, then put it in a buttered pan, and bake it in a brisk oven. Some people put currants in it.

To make a fine rich Cake.

Take two pounds of fresh butter beat to a cream, a pound of double refined sugar, a quartern and a half of fine flour, a pint of sweet wine, a quart of cream, five or six pounds of currants, a pint of yest, two nutmegs grated, some candied orange, lemon, and citron, a little orange flower water, some cinnamon, mace, ginger, and cloves; knead the whole well together, then put it into your hoop, and let it bake upwards of two hours.

A good Plumb Cake.

To a pound and an half of fine flour, add a pound of currants, half a pound of raisins stoned and chopped small, ten or twelve eggs (but only half the whites) a pound of butter worked to a cream, a gill of white wine or brandy, a pound of sugar, a little orange flower water, some candied citron, orange, and lemon, a few sweet almonds pounded, a little beaten mace, nutmeg, and cinnamon; when you have beat it all together about an hour, put in the hoop, and send it to the oven: it will take two hours baking.

Shrewsbury Cakes.

Take half a pound of fine flour, the same quantity of butter, beat up to a cream, one or two eggs, half a pound of loaf sugar beat and sifted, half an ounce of carraway seeds, and two spoonfuls of rose water; mix it all up into a paste, roll it thin, and cut it into little cakes, which must be laid on sheets of tin and sent to the oven.

To make Gingerbread Cakes.

You must take a pound of sugar, three pounds of flour, a pound of treacle made warm, some beaten mace, nutmeg, and ginger, a pound of melted butter, a gill of cream, a few coriander-seeds; mix all together to the consistence of a paste, roll it out and cut it into thin cakes, or roll it round in the shape of nuts. Let them be baked in a slack oven on tin plates.

To make Macaroons.

Take a pound of fine sugar, the whites of six or seven eggs, a pound of sweet almonds blanched and pounded, and a spoonful or two of rose water; beat all well together, shape your cakes on wafer-paper, grate a little sugar over them, and bake them on plates of tin.

To make Biscuits.

Take eight eggs well beaten, put to them a pound of fine powdered sugar, some grated lemon-peel, a little rose water, an ounce of coriander-seeds, and a pound of flour; mix the whole up together, shape it into biscuits

cuits on wafer paper, in whatever form you pleafe, duft fine fugar over them, and bake them.

To make good Pancakes.

Take eight yolks of eggs and four whites, a pint of cream or milk, three or four fpoonfuls of fack, a little fugar, a quarter of a pound of butter melted, half a pint of flour, fome grated nutmeg and falt; mix it all together, and pour as much of it into your frying-pan as will make one pancake; fhake the pan, and when one fide of the pancake is enough, turn it and do the other fide; then take it out, and fry the reft in the fame manner. When you difh them up, ftrew fugar over them.

To make good Fritters.

Add to a pint of thick cream five or fix beaten eggs but leave out three of the whites) a little brandy or fack, fome grated nutmeg, cinnamon, ginger, and falt; make this up into a thick batter with flour; then pare and chop a few golden pippins, mix them with the batter, and fry your fritters of a light brown in boiling lard: ferve them up with fugar fcattered over them. For change, you may put currants in the fritters.

CHAP. IX.

Of CHEESECAKES, CUSTARDS, CREAMS, SYLLABUBS, JELLIES, JAMS, &c.

To make fine Cheefecakes.

TAKE three quarters of a pound of butter melted, three or four ounces of fweet almonds blanched and beat fine, the curd of a gallon of new milk, three Naples bifcuits grated, the yolks of feven eggs, half a pound of currants, fome beaten cinnamon and nutmeg, half a pound of fine fugar, two or three fpoonfuls of fack, and a little rofe or orange flower water; mix all thefe well together, have ready fome patty-pans lined with

rich

rich cruſt, pour ſome of your mixture into each, and bake your cheeſecakes in a gentle oven.

To make Rice Cheeſecakes

To five or ſix ounces of rice boiled ſoft, add near half a pound of melted butter, ſix or ſeven ounces of loaf ſugar, h lf a nutmeg grated, four yolks of eggs beat up, a glaſs of brandy or ratifia, half a pint of cream or milk made warm, and a little cinnamon; beat all up together and bake the cheeſecakes in raiſed cruſts or patty-pans.

To make Lemon or Orange Cheeſecakes.

Firſt boil the rind of two large lemons or oranges, then pound it well in a mortar, with the yolks of half a dozen eggs, half a pound of butter beat to a cream, and about ſix ounces of fine ſugar; mix the whole up together, lay a thin puff-paſte in your patty-pans, pour into them your mixed ingredients, and ſet them in the oven.

To make common Cuſtards.

You muſt ſweeten a quart of cream or new milk to your palate; then grate in ſome nutmeg and cinnamon, beat up the yolks of eight eggs with a little roſe water, and ſtir them into your cream or milk; mix it up well, and bake it in cruſts or china cups: or you may put it into a deep china bowl, and ſet it in a kettle of boiling water, but do not let the water get into the bowl.

To make a Rice Cuſtard.

Boil a quart of cream with ſome ground rice, a little mace and nutmeg; ſtir it well together all the while it is boiling, and when it is enough ſweeten it to your taſte, and put in a little orange flower or roſe water. Serve it up either cold or hot.

Almond Cuſtards.

To a quarter of a pound of almonds blanched and pounded, add a quart of cream, two ſpoonfuls of roſe water,

water, the yolks of four or five eggs, some mace and cinnamon; mix it all together, sweeten it as you like, set it on the fire, and keep stirring it till it is of a proper thickness; then pour it into cups, and send it to table; or you may bake your almond custards in china cups.

To make Lemon or Orange Cream.

Take the juice of four large lemons or Seville oranges, half a pint of spring water, the whites of five or six eggs and the yolks of four well-beaten, a pint of cream boiled, and a pound of double refined sugar beat fine; mix the whole up well together, set it in a tossing pan over a gentle fire, put into it the peel of one orange or lemon, and keep stirring it one way all the time it is on the fire; when your cream is almost ready to boil, take out the peel, and pour the cream into china bowls, or jelly glasses.

Almond Cream.

First boil a quart of cream with a blade or two of mace, a piece of lemon-peel, and some grated nutmeg; then take four ounces of almonds blanched and beat very fine, the whites of eight or nine eggs well beaten, and a spoonful or two of rose water; mix these up with your cream, sweeten it to your taste, set it over the fire, stir it well till it is thick, and then pour it into glasses.

Whipt Cream.

Take the whites of eight eggs well beat, half a pint of sack, and a quart of good cream boiled; mix it all together, and sweeten it with fine sugar; whip it up with a whisk that has a piece of lemon-peel tied in the middle, skim off the froth, and put the mixture in glasses and basons.

To make a good Syllabub.

Having put a quart of cyder into a china bowl, grate a small nutmeg into it, and sweeten it with double refined sugar; then put into your liquor some new milk, fresh from the cow, and pour over that some nice cream.

To make a Whipt Syllabub.

To half a pint of Canary wine, add half a pound of fine sugar, the whites of three or four eggs, and a quart of cream; whip it up with a whisk till it froths; then skim it, and pour it into your syllabub glasses.

To make a Trifle.

Take a deep dish or bowl, cover the bottom with macaroons broke in two, ratafia cakes, and Naples biscuits broke in pieces; just moisten them with a little sack, then make a light boiled custard, and when it is cold put it over your macaroons, &c. and over that pour a fine syllabub.

To make a Currant Jelly.

First pick the currants from the stalks, then put them into a stone jar, cover it close, set it in a kettle of boiling water, and when it has boiled about half an hour, take it out, and strain off the juice of your currants; to every quart of juice add a pound and an half of loaf sugar, set it over a brisk clear fire, stir it gently till the sugar is melted, skim it well, and let it boil twenty minutes or half an hour; then pour your jelly into gallipots, cover each of the pots with paper dipped in brandy, and keep them for use in a dry place.

To make Hartshorn Jelly.

Take half a pound of hartshorn, put it into two quarts of spring water, and let it simmer over a moderate fire till the liquor is reduced to half the quantity, then strain it off, add to it the juice of two or three oranges and lemons, the whites of six eggs well beaten, a little Rhenish or white wine, some lemon-peel cut small, and nine or ten ounces of fine sugar; mix these up with your jelly, give it a boil, strain it through a jelly bag till it is clear, and then pour it into your jelly glasses.

To make Calves' Feet Jelly.

You must boil four calves' feet in a gallon of water till it is reduced to two quarts; then strain off the liquor

quor and let it ſtand till it is cold; ſkim off all the fat, clear the jelly from the ſediment, and put it in a ſaucepan, with eight whites of eggs beaten to a froth, a pint of Rheniſh or Madeira wine, a ſufficiency of loaf ſugar, the juice of four or five lemons, and ſome ſhred lemon-peel; ſtir all together, and let it boil up; then paſs it through your jelly bag till it is quite clear, and fill your glaſſes with it.

To make Raſberry Jam.

Bruiſe a quart of raſberries in a pint of currant jelly, boil them over a ſlow fire about twenty minutes, ſtir them all the time, and put ſome ſugar to them. When your jam is enough, pour it into your gallipots, cover it cloſe, and keep it for uſe.

To make Flummery.

Boil a large calf's foot in two quarts of water, then ſtrain the liquor, and put to it half a pint of thick cream, one ounce of bitter almonds, and two ounces of ſweet almonds well beat up together; ſweeten it with loaf ſugar; juſt give it a boil up, then ſtrain it off, and when cold put it into glaſſes or cups.

To make a good Sack Poſſet.

To a pint and a half of cream or new milk, add a little cinnamon or nutmeg, and two or three Naples biſcuits grated; let it boil over a ſlow fire till it is pretty thick, then put to it half a pint of ſack, with a ſufficiency of ſugar, ſtir it all together over the fire, and ſend it to table with dry toaſt.

To make Wine Whey.

You muſt put half a pint of white wine, and a pint of milk well ſkimmed, into a china bowl, and when it has ſtood a few minutes, pour a pint of hot water over it; let it ſtand till the curd ſettles at the bottom, then pour out the whey into another bowl, and mix ſugar with it.

CHAP.

CHAP. X.

Of PICKLING, PRESERVING, CANDYING, DRYING, POTTING, and COLLARING.

To pickle Mushrooms.

PUT the smallest mushrooms you can get into a pan of spring water, then rub them with a piece of flannel dipped in salt, and let them be well washed; set them on the fire in a stewpan of boiling spring water with a little salt in it, and when they have boiled five or six minutes, take them out, and throw them into a colander to drain; then lay them between two cloths till they are cold; after which put them into wide mouthed bottles, with a few blades of mace, some sliced nutmeg and mutton fat melted; fill up the bottles with distilled vinegar, cork them close and keep them for use.

To pickle Cabbage.

Having cut off the stalks and outside leaves, cut your cabbage in thin slices; meanwhile make a pickle of vinegar, salt, mace, ginger, cloves, and nutmeg, boil it, and pour it on your cabbage; then put it into stone jars, and cover them close.

To pickle Cucumbers.

Take some small cucumbers fresh gathered, put them in a pan, and pour over them some hot brine: let them stand twenty-four hours close covered, then strain them out into a colander, and dry them between two cloths. Take some white wine vinegar, and a proper quantity of allspice, boil it up, and then put your cucumbers into it, with a little salt and a few bay leaves; let them simmer over the fire in this pickle, then put the cucumbers and liquor into your jars, and tie a bladder over each.

To pickle Walnuts.

Put your walnuts in salt and water, in which they must remain several days, then take them out and dry them.

Of PRESERVING.

them. Boil some white wine vinegar with mace, cloves, pepper, ginger, nutmeg, and salt, pour it hot over your walnuts, and when they are cold, put them in strong stone jars.

To pickle Onions.

First peel some small onions, then soak them well in brine, and put them into wide-mouthed bottles, with sliced ginger, mace, bay leaves, and a little sweet oil; fill the bottles with white wine vinegar, and cork them up close.

To preserve Gooseberries, Cherries, Rasberries, Currants, Mulberries, &c.

Set your fruit over the fire, in a skillet or preserving pan, with a little water and a good deal of fine sugar; let it boil gently till the syrup is properly thick, then put your fruit and syrup into gallipots or glasses for use.

To keep Green Pease all the Year.

Having shelled some fine young pease, let them boil five or six minutes, then throw them into a colander to drain, dry them well with a cloth, and cover them close in quart bottles.

To Candy Orange or Lemon-Peel.

First steep your peel well in salt and water, then boil it tender, so as to take away the bitterness. Make a syrup of fine loaf sugar dissolved in water, put your peel into it, and boil it gently; then dry it before the fire, and keep it for use.

To candy Apricots.

Slit your apricots on one side of the stone, and put on them some fine sugar; lay them in a dish, and bake them in a pretty hot oven; then take them out of the dish and dry them on glass plates in the oven for two or three days.

To dry Peaches.

Having pared and stoned some fine large peaches, you must boil them tender; after which lay them in a sieve

sieve to drain, and put them in the saucepan again, with their weight of sugar; boil them till the syrup is thick enough, and let them lie in the sugar all night; then lay them on plates, and dry them thoroughly in a stove.

To dry Cherries.

Take a sufficiency of fine sugar, put a little water to it, and boil it; stone your cherries, put them in the sugar, give them a boil, and let them stand in the syrup two or three days; then boil your syrup again, and pour it on them: let them stand some time longer, then lay them in a sieve to dry.

To Pot Veal, Venison, Tongues, &c.

First bake or boil your meat, then cut it in very thin slices, and beat it well in a marble mortar, with some oily butter, a little mace, nutmeg, pepper, and salt; then put it down close in pots, pour clarified butter over it, and let it be kept in a dry place.

To Pot all kinds of Small Birds.

Having picked, drawn, and seasoned your birds, put them into a pot, lay butter over them, and set them in a moderate oven; when they are baked enough, take them out, drain the gravy from them, put them down close in your pots, and cover them with clarified butter. —N. B. You may pot fish in the same manner, but take care to bone them.

To collar Pork.

Take a breast of pork, bone it, and season it well with pepper, salt, spice, thyme, sage, and parsley; roll it up tight in a coarse cloth, and boil it in water and vinegar; then take it out of the cloth, and keep it in the same liquor in which you boiled it.

To collar Beef.

Take a piece of salted beef, beat it well, rub it over with yolks of eggs, season it with mace, salt, pepper, cloves, nutmeg, thyme, parsley, marjorum, and savory; then

then roll it into a hard collar, bind it round with coarse broad tape, and boil it in spring water, with some red wine and cochineal. When it is cold, take off the tape, and keep your beef in the liquor it was boiled in.

To callar a Breast of Veal, or a Pig.

Having boned your pig or veal, season it with savory spice and sweet herbs, roll it up tight, bind it with tape, wrap it in a clean cloth, and boil it tender in vinegar and water, with a few cloves, some mace, salt, pepper, sweet herbs, and a slice or two of lemon. When cold, take it out of the cloth, put it with the liquor in an earthen pan, and keep it close covered.

To collar Mutton.

Bone a breast of mutton, season it with mace, nutmeg, cloves, salt, pepper, sweet herbs, shred lemon-peel, the yolks of eggs, anchovies, and grated bread; roll it up into a collar, bind it tight with coarse tape, and either boil, roast, or bake it.

To collar Eels.

Scour your eels with salt, slit them down the back, bone them, wash and dry them, season them with mace, nutmeg, pepper, salt, parsley, sage, and thyme; then roll them up in cloths, tie them close, and boil them in water and salt, with a pint of vinegar, a bunch of sweet herbs, and some spice. When they are boiled, strain the pickle, and keep your eels in it for use.

To make a Ham.

First cut a fine ham off a fat hind-quarter of pork; then take a pound of coarse sugar, an ounce and a half of salt-petre, and a pound of common salt, mix these up together, and rub your ham well with it; let it lie in this pickle near a month, turn and baste it every day, then hang it in wood smoke for several days, and, after that, hang it up in a cool dry place.

To make Bacon.

Take all the inside fat off a side of pork, rub your pork over with salt, and let it lie a week; then wipe it clean, rub it well with a little salt-petre, some coarse sugar, and common salt, lay it in this pickle for about a fortnight, turn and baste it every day, then hang it in wood smoke as you do the ham; after which hang it up to dry in a place that is cool.

CHAP. XI.

Of ENGLISH WINES and OTHER LIQUORS.

To make Currant Wine.

LET your currants be gathered when perfectly ripe; strip them from the stalks, put them in a large pan with some water and bruise them with a wooden pestle; let them stand in the pan twenty-four hours, then strain off the liquor. To every gallon of this liquor add three pounds of loaf sugar, and to every six gallons put a quart of brandy; stir it well together, put it in a cask, and let it stand three or four months, then bottle it off for use.

To make Raisin Wine.

First boil nine or ten gallons of spring water for an hour, then put six pounds of Malaga raisins to every gallon; let them remain in the water about ten days, and you must stir them every day; then strain the liquor off, squeeze the juice out of the raisins, mix both liquors well together, and put your wine in a barrel; stop it up close, let it stand about four months, and then put it in bottles.

To make Gooseberry Wine.

Bruise your gooseberries in a tub with a mallet, squeezing out all the juice, and put to it a sufficient quantity of water and loaf sugar; mix it up well till the sugar

sugar is melted, then put it into a cask, and when it has stood three or four months, bottle it off, putting a small lump of sugar in each bottle.

To make Orange Wine.

Take six whites of eggs well beat, fifteen pounds of loaf sugar, and six gallons of spring water; boil all together about three quarters of an hour, and take off the scum as it rises. When it is cold, mix with it five or six spoonfuls of yest, five ounces of the syrup of lemon or citron, and the juice and rinds of between thirty and forty oranges; let it work two days, then put it into a cask with one quart of Rhenish or Mountain wine, and after two or three months bottle it off.

To make Good English Sack.

To every gallon of water put a handful of fennel roots, and to every quart a sprig of rue; let these boil half an hour, then strain off the liquor, and add to every gallon three pounds of honey; boil it about two hours, and clear it of scum. When cold, turn it into a cask, and after it has stood several months bottle it.

To make Shrub.

Take half a gallon of brandy, add to it a pint of new milk, the juice of six lemons or Seville oranges, and the rinds of three; let it stand twenty four hours, then put to it a pound and a half of fine sugar, and three pints of white wine; mix it up well, strain it through a flannel bag till it is clear, and bottle it for use.

To make Rasberry Brandy.

Bruise a quantity of rasberries, and strain the juice from them; to each quart of juice put a quart of good brandy; then boil some water with a sufficiency of double refined sugar, and mix it with brandy and rasberry juice; stir it well together, and let it stand in a stone jar, close covered, above a month; then pour it off into your bottles.

To make Cherry Brandy.

Stone and mash eight pounds of black cherries, and put to them three quarts or a gallon of the best brandy; sweeten it to your palate, cover it up close in a proper vessel, and when it has stood a month, clear it of the sediment and bottle it off.

To make excellent Milk Punch.

Take a quart of new milk, a quart of brandy, half a pint of lemon juice, two quarts of warm water, and some sugar; mix all together, strain it through a flannel bag, and bottle it. This will keep upwards of a fortnight.

CHAP. XII.
COMPLETE INSTRUCTIONS FOR MARKETING.

How to choose Beef.

IF the beef be young, it will be smooth and tender; if old, it generally appears rough and spungy. When it is of a carnation colour, it is a sign of its being good spending meat.

To choose Mutton.

When mutton is old, the flesh, when pinched, will wrinkle and continue so; if it be young, the flesh will pinch tender, and the fat will easily part from the lean; whereas when the meat is old, the fat will stick by strings and skins. The flesh of ewe mutton is in general paler than that of wether mutton; it is of a closer grain, and parts more easily. When the flesh of mutton is loose at the bone, and of a pale yellowish colour, it is an indication of its being somewhat rotten.

To choose Lamb.

If a hind quarter of lamb has a faint smell under the kidney, and the knuckle be limber, it is stale meat. If the neck vein of a fore-quarter be of an azure colour, it is new and good meat; but if greenish or yellowish, the meat is nearly tainted.

To choose Pork.

If the pork be old, the lean will be tough, and the fat spungy and flabby; if young, the lean, when pinched, will break between your fingers, and when you nip the skin with your nails, it will make a dent. The skin of pork is in general clammy and sweaty when the meat is stale, but smooth and cool when new. When many little kernels, like hail-shot, are found in the fat of pork, it is then measly.

To choose Veal.

When the flesh of a joint of veal seems clammy, and has greenish or yellowish specks, it is stale; but when it has not these appearances it is new. The flesh of a female calf is not so red and firm as that of a male calf.

To choose Bacon.

If the fat is white, oily to the touch, and does not break, the bacon is good, especially if the flesh is of a good colour and sticks well to the bone; but if contrary symptoms appear, and the lean has some yellowish streaks, it is or soon will be rusty.

To choose Hams.

You must run a knife under the bone that sticks out of the ham, and if it comes out pretty clean, and has a nice flavour, the ham is sweet and good; if much dulled and smeared, it is tainted and rancid.

To choose Venison.

In a haunch or shoulder of venison, put your finger or knife under the bones that stick out, and as the smell is rank or sweet, it is stale or new.

To choose Turkeys, Capons, Geese, Ducks, &c.

If the turkey be young, its legs will be smooth and black, and its spurs short; if it be stale, its eyes will be sunk, and feet dry; if new, the eyes will be lively, and the feet limber.

When a cock or capon is young, his spurs are short and his legs smooth; if stale, he will have a loose open vent; if new, a close hard vent.

If the bill of a goose is yellowish, and she has but few hairs she is young; but if her bill and feet are reddish, and she has plenty of hairs, she is an old one. If the goose be fresh, the feet will be limber; if stale, they will be dry.

Wild and tame ducks, if stale will be dry footed; if fresh limber footed.

To choose Hares and Rabbits.

A hare when newly killed, is stiff and whitish; when stale, the body is limber, and the flesh in many parts blackish. If the hare be old, the ears will be tough and dry, and the claws wide and ragged; if young, the claws will be smooth, and the ears will tear like a piece of brown paper. Rabbits, when stale, are limber and slimy; when fresh, stiff and white; when young, their claws are smooth; when old, the contrary.

To choose Salmon, Carp, Tench, Pike, Trout, Whitings, Barbels, Smelts, Shads, Chubs, Ruffs, Mackarel, Herrings, &c.

When these fish are stale, their gills are pale, their flesh soft and clammy, and their eyes dull and sunk; but when fresh, the gills are of a lively shining redness, the eyes bright and full, and flesh stiff.

CHAP. XIII.
MODERN BILLS OF FARE.

A Bill of Fare for an elegant Entertainment, in the Order in which the Dishes should be placed upon the Table.

First Course.

	Dish of Fish	
Rabbits with Onions		Collared Mutton
Pigeon Pie raised	Gravy Soup	Almond Pudding
Veal Cutlets	Roast Beef	Ham or Tongue

Second

Of BILLS OF FARE.

Second Course.

Green Peafe or Afparagus	Roafted Turkey.	Prawns
Ragout of Sweetbreads	Jellies and Syllabubs	Fried Smelts
Tanfey		Mufhrooms
	Chickens roafted	

Third Course.

Artichoke Bottoms	Blomange	Stewed Celery
Almond Cheefecakes	A Trifle	Cuftards
Lemon Cakes	Sweetmeats	Fruit

Another Bill of Fare arranged in the moft genteel Order.

First Course.

Chickens	Turbot	Ox-palates
Lamb Pie	Mock Turtle	Ham
Scotch Collops		Orange Pudding
	Chine of Mutton	

Second Course.

Lamb's Fry	Wild Fowls	Sturgeon
Lobfters roafted	Jellies	Apple Pie
Crawfifh		Artichokes
	A Hare roafted	

A Third Bill of Fare, properly arranged.
First Course.

	Stewed Carp, or Tench	
Fillet of Pork		Sheeps rumps
Beef Steak Pie	Vermicelli Soup	Ham
Veal Olives		Calves Ears
	Two Fowls boiled	

Second Course.

	Green Goose	
Asparagus		Crawfish
Gooseberry Tarts	A Trifle	Custards
Prawns		Scotch Collops
	Tame Pigeons	

A Fourth Bill of Fare, with seven Dishes in each Course.
First Course.

	Haunch of Venison	
Pigeon Pie		Lemon Pudding
	Cod's Head	
Chickens with Oysters		Lamb Cutlets
	Ragout of Veal	

Second Course.

	Brace of Partridges	
Spitchcocked Eels		Artichokes
	Wild Ducks or Teals	
Cream Tarts		Buttered Apple Pie.
	Smelts	

CHAP. XIV.

DIRECTIONS CONCERNING CLEAR-STARCHING.

How to wash Muslin Aprons, Neckcloths, Hoods, &c.

LET your muslins be folded four times double, putting the two selvages together, then the ends together, and wash them the way the selvage goes, to prevent their fraying. Take very clear water, not too hot, and strain it through a clean cloth into a pan; then take some of the best soap, put it upon a clean stick, and beat up your lather; after the lather is beat, put in your muslins one by one, and let them stand to soak out the dirt; then wash them one by one to prevent tearing, whilst the water is warm; squeeze them very hard between both your hands, that the dirty suds may not be left in them; and as you wash them out, shake them open into another pan. Then beat up your second lather, wash your muslins in it, and squeeze them as before. As to your third lather let the water be very hot, but not boiling, for that makes the water yellow; then take a small quantity of powder-blue, put it in a cup and add to it a little water; shake the cup about, pour the powder-blue into the hot water, and stir it about till it is blue enough; then take some soap, beat up your lather as before, put in your muslins, and let them be covered with a clean cloth. You may either wash them out whilst warm, or let them stand all night to clear.

You must observe, when you wash them out, to wash out the blue carefully; then lay them in spring water, and if you have not time to starch them all at once, you need not put any more in your starch than you can finish in one day; for if they lie too long in the starch, it makes them look yellow and streaky. Many clear-starchers boil their muslins, but they should not, because it wears them out the sooner; but the scalding and letting the muslins lie in warm suds, does them more good than a boil.

Of CLEAR STARCHING.

The Method of rinsing Muslins before Starching.

First put some spring water in a clean pan, then take a little powder-blue in a cup, add a spoonful or two of water to it, shake it about in the cup, and pour a little of it into the rinsing water, then put your hand in the rinsing water, and stir it about; put your whitest muslins in first, one by one, squeezing them out separately as you put them in, and if any blue should settle upon them, rub them gently in the water with your hand, and it will come off; and if any of your muslins should happen to be yellow, you must make the rinsing water a little bluer. When you have rinsed them all out, squeeze them very hard, one by one, between your hands, because they will not take the starch so well if any water is left in them; and having pulled them out separately with very dry hands, double them up, and lay them upon a dry clean cloth in order to be starched.

How to starch the Muslins.

To a quarter of a pound of starch, take a pint of spring water; put the water in a skillet, and set it over a clear fire till it is lukewarm; then put in your starch, stir it gently one way till it boils one boil and no more; pour it into a clean pan, and cover it with a plate till it is cold; when cold, take some of it in one hand, and some blue in the other, and mix them together, but do not make it too blue. Take up your muslins one by one, and spread the starch with your hand, but not too thick, first on one side and then on the other, without opening them; then blue the finest muslins first, and the thickest afterwards, for the starch that comes out of the finest will serve for the thick ones. When you have starched your muslins, lay them in the same pan, kneading them with your double fist till the starch sticks about your hands; then wring them very hard, and wipe them with a dry cloth; after which you must open them, and rub them very lightly through your hands.

How to clap the Muslins.

After you have unfolded your muslins, and rubbed them through your hands, take the two ends and clap them

them hard between your hands; then pull them out very well with both hands, to you and from you, to prevent their fraying. Let your hands be exceeding dry; for if any starch remains on the hands, it will fray the muslins; dry them well, and as you pull them out, hold them up against the light, to see if they are clapped enough. If you observe any thing that looks shining, that is the starch, you must rub it over gently with your hands; when they are clapped sufficiently, you will observe them to fly asunder, and not stick to the hands. Take care to clap very quick and hard, and when you see no shining on them, they are clapped enough. They ought never to be clapped single, for that frays and tears them; neither should they be clapped by the fire except in cold frosty weather.

To iron the Muslins.

When you find they are sufficiently clapped, pull them out double on your ironing board, as smooth and as even as possible, and so on till you have finished about six, one upon another; then take a box-iron, and iron the driest first. Let fine plain muslins be ironed upon a soft woollen cloth; but if you have any muslins that are thick and coarse, let them be first ironed on a damp cloth, and afterwards upon your ironing cloth, on the wrong side of the muslins.

To wash and starch Lawns Cambrick, &c.

You may wash and rinse lawns in the same manner as muslins; dip them in thin starch, and squeeze them out hard, wipe them with a dry cloth, and clap them very carefully, because they are apt to slip. When clapped enough, fold them up, and put them into a clean dry pan; do not touch them with any wet, for that will leave a kind of thick look upon them, as well as on muslins. They may be ironed on a damp cloth, but not with an iron that is too hot; and you may iron them on the wrong side as you do the coarse muslins.

Excellent Methods of taking Iron Moulds, Stains of Ink, Claret, &c. out of Muslins, Table Linen, &c.

Whenever your muslins, linen, &c. happen to be

iron-moulded, take a chafing-difh of clear coals, and fet over it a plate with forrel in it; then put a little falt to the forrel, and lay the ftained part upon the plate; afterwards take fome more forrel, and fqueeze the juice over the ftained muflin or linen; let it lie till it is very hot, and take the ftained part and fqueeze it hard; then take frefh forrel and falt, and make ufe of it as before, till the iron moulds are entirely out; you muft then immediately wafh the ftained part in three or four lathers, to take out the greennefs.

If your muflins or linen are ftained by claret, take fome milk, make it very warm, and foak the ftained parts in it till the ftains are quite out. When your linens are ftained by ink, let them lie all night in vinegar and falt; the next day rub the ftains well with it; then take frefh vinegar and falt, and let your linen lie in it another night; the next morning rub it again, and the fpots will immediately difappear.

If there be any ftains of fruit in your muflins or linen, rub the fpots well with butter, then put the ftained part of the linen or muflin into hot milk, in which let it lie till it is cold; then rub the ftains in the milk till they are quite gone away.

CHAP. XV.

A COLLECTION OF PHYSICAL RECEIPTS.

For an Afthma. YOU may drink a pint of fea water every morning; or a fpoonful of nettle juice, mixed with clarified honey.

For an Ague. Take a drachm of powder of myrrh, mixed with a fpoonful of fack, and drink a glafs of fack after it. Let this be done about an hour before the fits come on. Dr. MEAD.

For the King's Evil. You may take every morning and evening, as much cream of Tartar as will lie on a fixpence.

For the Scurvy. Infufe dried dock-roots in your common drink; or pound into a pulp an equal quantity
of

of fine sugar and sliced Seville Oranges, and take a tea-spoonful of it three or four times a day. Dr. Buchan says, the most proper drink in the scurvy is whey or butter milk.

For the Quinsey. Swallow the juice or jelly of black currants.

For the Hooping-Cough, or Chin-Cough. Take a spoonful of the juice of penny-royal two or three times a day, mixed with honey or sugar candy.

For the Head-Ach. Let your head be washed with cold water for a quarter of an hour; or you may snuff up your nose the juice of ground-ivy.

For the Ear-Ach. Apply the ear close to the mouth of a jug filled with warm water, or with a strong decoction of camomile flowers. Dr. BUCHAN.

For the Rheumatism. You may use the cold bath, with rubbing and sweating after it.

For the itch. Let the parts affected be washed with a strong decoction of dock-roots, for eight or ten days; or steep a shirt half an hour in a quart of water mixed with half an ounce of powdered brimstone, dry it slowly, and wear it six or seven days.

For the Pleurisy. Drink a glass of tar-water warm, twice every hour.

For a Sore Throat. Gargle with rose-water and syrup of mulberries; or apply a chin-stay of roasted figs.

For the Colic. Apply externally a bag of hot oats; or take from fifty to an hundred drops of oil of aniseed on a lump of sugar.

For the Tooth-Ach. Put into the hollow tooth a little cotton dipped in Luceteilis balsam, or in oil of cloves.

For expelling Worms. Take two or three tea-spoonfuls of worm seed mixed with treacle, for five or six mornings.

For the Dropsy. Every morning and evening take a spoonful or two of the juice of artichoke leaves, or the juice of leeks and elder leaves; or take a drachm of nitre every morning in a draught of ale.

For the Gravel. Drink plentifully of warm water sweetened with honey.

For the Stone. Take a tea-spoonful of calcined onions in a glass of white wine.

For a consumptive Cough. Stone ten or twelve raisins of the sun, and fill them up with the small tender tops of rue; take them early every morning, and fast for two or three hours afterwards.

An excellent Eye-Water. Infuse in lime-water for twelve hours, a drachm of sal ammoniac powdered; then strain it and keep it for use. This cures most disorders of the eye.

For the Lethargy. You may snuff strong vinegar up the nose.

For the Palsy. Shred some white onions, and bake them gently in an earthen pot till they are soft; spread a thick plaister of this, and apply it to the benumbed part.

For the Stranguary. You may drink largely of a decoction of turnips sweetened with honey *.

CHAP. XVI.

VARIOUS RECEIPTS for PRESERVING and IMPROVING BEAUTY.

To make a fine Pomatum for the Skin.

HAVING cut two pounds of hog's lard into thin slices, wash it clean, and let it soak in cold water eight or ten days, changing the water once a day; then melt it over a slow fire, and skim off any impurity that rises to the top; when melted pour it into cold water, wash it clean with rose-water, and then rub your skin with it.

To remove Freckles.

Mix three or four spoonfuls of bean flower water with the same quantity of elder flower water, and add a

---

* I have thus selected some approved remedies for the most common disorders incident to the human body; but I would most earnestly recommend to my readers that *most valuable Library of Family Medicines,* Dr. GORDON's COMPLETE ENGLISH PHYSICIAN, It being the best book of the kind now extant.

spoonful

spoonful of oil of tartar; when the mixture has stood two or three days, and is properly settled, rub a little over your face, and let it dry upon it.

To take off red Spots from the Face.

Place a lemon before a slow fire, in a flat earthen plate, to receive the liquor that sweats out of it; when all the juice is out, pour it into a glass to cool, and then rub the face with a few drops of it. This is an effectual method of removing all kinds of red spots.

To remove Wrinkles.

Take two ounces of the powder of myrrh, and lay it in a small fire-shovel till it is thoroughly hot; then take a mouthful of white wine, and let it fall gently upon the myrrh, which will smoke up; you must then immediately hold your face over it, so as to receive as much of the smoke as possible; if you hold your face over till the whole is wasted, it will have a wonderful effect; but if that is too painful you may cover your face with a cloth.

To take away Spots from the Nails.

Take two drachms of Venice Turpentine and one drachm of myrrh, mix them together over a slow fire in an earthen vessel, and then let the mixture cool; spread a small piece of it upon leather, and keep it all night upon your nails; let this be continued for three nights, and the spots will disappear.

To conceal deep Marks occasioned by the Small Pox.

You must boil an ounce of spermaceti in a pint of Malmsey till it is entirely dissolved; add to it the juice of a house-leek and that of plaintain leaves, with half an ounce of peach kernels: when it is all well mixed together, you must set it to cool; then strain it through a fine cloth, and when you rub your face with it let it be gently warmed.

To make a fine washing Powder.

Take three or four ounces of the flower of French barley, two ounces of the oil of sweet almonds, six drachms of benjamin, a handful of the leaves of white roses,

roses, half an ounce of spermaceti, an ounce of white chalk powdered, a quarter of an ounce of white tartar, and one scruple of the oil of cloves and lavender; mix all these together, and beat them to powder in a mortar.

To make a Perfume to carry in your Pocket.

Take two scruples of the flowers of benjamin, half a scruple of the flowers of roses, one scruple of orange-peel, some grated nutmeg, a scruple of the essence of cinnamon and orange, half an ounce of jessamine butter, and a few grains of musk and amber; beat all these in a morter till they are properly mixed, then put the powder in a box.

To make fine Wash Balls.

Mix two ounces of sanders with the same quantity of cloves, four pounds of the best white soap cut in small pieces, and twenty grains of musk; dissolve the whole in rose-water, and then make it up into balls.

To make the Hands soft and white.

First beat in a mortar two ounces of blanched almonds, with four ounces of the flowers of beans; add to them four ounces of Castile soap, with a pint of rose water; then mix them all up together, and when you use them for your hands, moisten them with warm milk.

To make an excellent wash for the Teeth.

Mix an ounce of bole-armoniac in a gill of Hungary water; put this into a quart of claret, with two ounces of honey, a drachm of allum, an ounce of myrrh, and ten grains of salt of vitriol; then let this mixture stand to settle. When you use it, put a spoonful of it into a cup of water, wash your teeth with it every morning, and it will preserve them clean and white.

To make a swarthy Complexion appear agreeable.

First sift the flour out of half a peck of wheat bran; then put to the bran seven or eight new-laid eggs, and six pints of white-wine vinegar; when it is well mixed up, let it distil over a slow fire. After it has stood a day to settle, rub your face with it every day for a fortnight, and then it will look extremely fair.

INDEX.

INDEX.

A
Artichokes, to boil, 21
Asparagus, to boil, ib.

B
Bacon, to make, 88
Beans, to boil, 22
Beef to boil, 13—to roast, 24—to stew, 40—to hash, 45—to bake, 47—to fricassee, 48
Beef Steaks, to broil, 33—to fry, 35—to stew, 39
Birds, to pot, 86
Biscuits, to make, 78
Brandy, to make, rasberry and cherry brandy, 89, 90
Broccoli, to boil, 21
Broths, to make, 64
Bullock's Heart, to bake, 47

C
Cabbage to pickle, 84
Cakes, to make, 77 to 79
Calf's head, to dress, 15. 46, 47
Calf's liver, to roast, 27—to fry, 38
Calf's feet to fricassee, 50
Candies, to make, 85
Carp, to dress, 20. 38. 44
Cauliflower, to dress, 20
Cheesecakes, to make, 79
Chickens, to dress, 16. 29. 33—to force, 56
Clear Starching, 95
Cod, to dress, 19. 34. 43
Cod's Head, to bake or roast, 57
Cod-founds, to broil, 34
Creams, to make, 81
Cucumbers, to ragoo, 59—to pickle, 84
Custards, to make, 80

D
Ducks, to dress, 16. 30. 56. 62

E
Eels, to dress, 20. 31. 34. 39. 44
Eggs to fricassee, 51

F
Fish to bake, 48—to fricassee, 51
Flounders, to dress, 19. 38. 44
Forcemeat Balls for Made-Dishes, 59
Fowls, to dress, 17. 29

G
Gibles, to stew, 42
Goose, to dress, 16. 29. 42
Gravies, to make, 62, 63

H
Ham, to boil, 15—to make, 87
Hare, to dress, 28. 41. 56
Herrings, to dress, 35. 38

I
Instructions for Marketing, 90 to 92
Jam, rasberry, to make, 93
Jellies, to make, 82, 83

L
Lamb, to boil, 14—to roast, 25—to fry, 36—to fricassee, 49—to ragoo, 54
Lamb's Head, to dress, 54
Lamb's Pits, to dress, 55
Lampreys, to fry, 39
Larks, to roast, 30
Leg of beef, to bake, 47
Lobster, to roast, 32

M
Mackarel, to dress, 19, 37
Mock Turtle, to dress, 58

Modern

INDEX.

Modern Bills of Fare, 92 to 94
Muscles to stew, 45
Mushrooms to fricassee, 51
—to pickle 84
Mutton, to boil. 14—to roast, 23—to fry, 36—to stew, 40—to hash, 45—to bake, 47—to ragoo 52

N
Neat's Tongues, to fricassee 49

O
Onions, to pickle, 85
Oysters, to stew, 45
Ox Palates, to stew, 40

P
Parsnips to boil 21
Partridges or Pheasants, to dress, 18. 30. 43
Pease, green, to boil, 24
Pease, to keep green all the year, 85
Pies, to make, 72 to 76
Pig, to dress, 26. 41. 48. 50
Pigs Pettitoes, to dress, 55
Pigs Feet and Ears, to ragoo 55
Pigeons, to dress, 16, 17. 30, 33. 42. 50. 56
Pike. to roast, 31
Pork, to boil, 14—to roast, 25
Puddings to make, 68 to 72

Q
Quails, to roast, 31

R
Rabbits, to dress, 17, 18, 27. 41. 46. 50
Ragout for Made Dishes 60
Receipts, Physical, 98, 99

Receipts for preserving Beauty, 100, 101, 102

S
Salmon, to dress, 20. 34
Sauces, to make, 65 to 67
Sausages to fry, 37
Scate, to dress, 18
Scotch Collops, to make 37
Snipes, to boil, 17—to roast, 31—to ragoo, 57
Soups, to make, 60 to 62
Spinach, to boil, 21
Sturgeon, to dress, 18. 31. 59
Sweetbreads and Kidneys, to fry, 37—to ragoo, 54
Syllabubs, to make, 81, 82

T
Tarts, to make, 72
Tench, to dress, 20. 38. 44
Tongues to dress, 14. 26. 33
Tripe, to fry, 37
Trout, to dress, 38. 44
Turbot, to boil, 19
Turkey, to dress, 25. 28. 42 —to roast with chesnuts 29
Turtle, to dress, 57
Turnips, to boil, 22

V
Veal to boil, 13—to roast, 24—to ragoo, 53—to pot and collar, 86
Veal Cutlets, to fry, 36
Venison, to boil, 14—to roast, 27—to hash, 46—to ragoo, 55

W
Walnuts, to pickle, 84
Wines, English, to make, 88, 89, 90
Woodcocks, to roast, 31— to ragoo, 57

FINIS.